By Denis Waitley

Seeds of Greatness
The Double Win

DENIS WAITLEY

THE DOUBLE WIN

Fleming H. Revell Company
Old Tappan, New Jersey

Excerpts from *In Search of Excellence: Lessons From America's Best-Run Companies* by Thomas J. Peters and Robert H. Waterman, Jr., Copyright © 1982 by Thomas J. Peters and Robert H. Waterman, Jr. Reprinted by permission of Harper & Row, Publishers, Inc.

Material from Celestial Seasonings Beliefs used by permission.

Excerpt from *Pygmalion* used by permission of The Society of Authors on behalf of the Bernard Shaw Estate.

Excerpt from "ITT: The Giant Slumbers," by Leslie Wayne, Copyright © 1984 by The New York Times Company. Reprinted by permission.

Quotations from *Me: The Narcissistic American,* by Aaron Stern, M.D., Copyright © 1979 by Ballantine Books, a division of Random House, Inc. Used by permission.

Excerpt from "On Children" from *The Prophet,* by Kahlil Gibran, Copyright © 1972 by Alfred A. Knopf, Inc. Used by permission.

Library of Congress Cataloging in Publication Data
Waitley, Denis.
    The double win.

    Bibliography: p.
    1. Success.   I. Title.
BJ1611.2.W35   1985   158'.1   84-17903
ISBN 0-8007-1227-7

TO Susan, who lives a Double Win life and
always gives without question

Acknowledgments

My special appreciation goes to Michael Wolf, Ph.D., who has made a major contribution to this work. Dr. Wolf is a real talent in the field of high-performance human achievement. His Double Win attitude in contributing source data and substance has been invaluable and indispensable to me.

Thanks also to Fritz Ridenour, my editor, whose patience, hours of effort, gentle prodding, and, most of all— creativity—finally got the job done.

Also, my gratitude to my friend and associate Martin Carmichael, who, during our twenty-year odyssey of valleys and peaks, has never stopped converting every stumbling block into a stepping-stone.

And my thanks to Lee and Bette, for always giving but never giving up.

Contents

Winning Is Giving

Winning is giving your best self away
Winning is serving with grace every day
You'll know that you've won when your friends say it's true.
"I like who I am, when I'm around you.
You look for the best in the others you see
And you help us become who we're trying to be."

Winning is helping someone who's down
It's sharing a smile instead of a frown.

It's giving your children a hug by the fire
And sharing the values and dreams that inspire.

It's giving your parents the message "I care.
Thanks, Mom and Dad, for being so fair."

Winners are willing to give more than get
Their favors are free, you're never in debt.

Winning is giving one hundred percent
It's paying your dues, your taxes, your rent
It's trying and doing, not crying and stewing.

Winners respect every color and creed
They share and they care for everyone's need.

The losers keep betting that winning is getting
But there's one of God's laws that they keep forgetting
And this is the Law you can live and believe
The more that you give, the more you'll receive!

Prologue: What the monarch butterfly taught me . . .

Anne Morrow Lindbergh was right after all. She had cautioned in the opening reflections of her classic book *Gift From the Sea* that the beach was not a place to work or write, but rather a place to patiently wait and find some gifts of self-discovery.

Susan and I had come to our hideaway at Sea Ranch, armed with a canvas bag full of notes, magazine clippings, and a variety of recent best-sellers on the subject of value clarification, motivation, and management. My plan was to put the finishing touches on this book, inspired by the sounds and smells of the surf and by the sights of fauna, flora, and a hundred Jonathan Livingston Seagulls gliding effortlessly above the rugged cliffs of the northern California coastline.

That was my plan. But, prophetically, I sat and stared out to sea, hypnotized by the immensity and sheer elegance of God's artistry. Instead of answers for my readers, I found more questions for myself.

Are the whales really frolicking or are they merely ridding themselves of barnacles and parasites as they roll on the sandy bottom—just offshore—with giant flukes saluting us as they pass in review?

Why do cormorants fly out over the waves, bank sharply, and fly back, repeating this maneuver over and over again? Are they on early-warning patrol or simply neurotic?

Did early settlers plant the yellow daffodils, calla lilies, white

15

daisies, and persimmon-colored poppies, rosy beach morning glories and blue wild iris? Or were they always there?

How do millions of orange-and-black monarch butterflies survive the two-thousand-mile migration from the hidden forests of Mexico to our seaside garden on such fragile wings? How do they navigate? And why make the arduous journey at all?

How do we humans survive and navigate through such tumultuous winds of revolution and change? What drives us?

Why are we so emotionally fragile and susceptible to environmental whim and external stimulation?

Is success measurable or is it like the monarch butterfly—always on the wing?

When a butterfly is caught, pinned down, and put on display, there is a kind of sadness in the ceremony. There is a certain selfish reward in the possession of something so exquisite. But there is a longing to experience the exhilaration again, found only in the flutter of shared "aliveness."

Maybe I was overcomplicating my theory of success and the Double Win. Maybe in my attempt to serve both corporate and personal objectives, I was actually creating the "Double Bind" instead of the "Double Win." Maybe the concepts of giving and getting were truly incompatible.

As I brushed the sand off my jeans and started back up the path from the tidal pools to our house, I picked a wild blackberry and popped it in my mouth. The delightful taste immediately provoked a sensory flashback to my grandma's garden. Another monarch darted into view and paused in a morning glory bed, wings still in motion, like a marathoner sipping fluids along the way. I wondered if perhaps the sun had made me a trifle light-headed and giddy in considering the analogy of "winning" and "winging" in life. Butterflies, Olympic competition, and Fortune 500 bottom-line goals, all in the same thought process? Preposterous! Or was it?

I removed my wet Adidas on the redwood deck and went through the sliding-glass doors directly into my study. There, mocking me, was the huge green eye of my impersonal but impetuous word processor, hungry for input. On my last attempt at typing and storing my manuscript via this technological marvel, a power surge in Mendocino County had zapped four of my most prolific pages of text and beamed them off into space with Spock, E.T., and Luke Skywalker.

I pushed the power-on switch and muttered under my breath, "I'm with Andy Rooney. Give me my old Underwood manual anytime. At least we understand each other!"

If only Kim and Lisa, my teenage daughters, were there to help. Computers were old hat to them.

"Where are those kids when I need them most?" I snorted. "Probably getting blackberry stains on their hands or watching coastal seals bleaching in the sun on the rocks. Why aren't they dutifully at my side to help figure out how to get into this confounded Wordstar software program? How can I etch my wordprints on the sands of time when I still have trouble with giving this thing basic commands like 'cursor to home'?"

The obvious pun was not lost upon me. This green-eyed monster could make anybody curse! How did a hopeless romantic like me, who grew up on Sandburg, De Mille, and manual typewriters end up with kids weaned on Speilberg, Lucas, and Apple II?

I shrugged and vowed that frustration would not spoil the mood of inspiration that had come to me on the beach. The monarch butterfly had taught me with a powerful parable. I knew winning was simple but not at all easy. I wasn't trying to capture the concept of the Double Win in some pat formula, but I did want to set the secret free so others could share in the experience.

As I thought of you—the reader—I began to get in touch. Slowly the blank emerald screen began filling with words and phrases.

Is it possible to reconcile the seemingly hopeless conflict between winning by competition and comparison and winning by creating and cooperation?

Can the Double Win be applied to business and sports as well as family and personal relationships? Can the Golden Rule be applied in a world of bullion and petrodollars?

Can we really get the most out of life by giving the most to others?

I believe we can, and the pages that follow will tell you why.

PART I

What Is the Double Win?

When I talk about the Double Win many people give me quizzical, sometimes even suspicious, looks. How can *both* sides win? Isn't life a game with winners and losers? You win some, you lose some. It's the law of nature—simple as that.

But is it?

I don't think so.

Yes, the win-lose approach has been around a long time.

Yes, the win-lose approach is still overwhelmingly popular. But there is another way. It is called win-win—the Double Win. And it works.

1

Today's Winning Warp

The first question we may need to deal with is:

"Why *another* book on winning? Doesn't the avalanche of self-help books on success reflect an idea whose time has come and gone?"

I disagree, but I can understand the disillusionment and growing boredom. Any number of best-selling book titles have produced slogans like:

"Look out for Number One."
"Win by intimidation."
"Have it all."
"You can achieve success!"

The never-ending stream of books, tapes, and films on gaining the good life seem to prompt several basic responses. In the course of my public-speaking travels (which I do to tell people how to succeed and win) I log something like seven hundred thousand miles a year. Everywhere I go I find these typical reactions:

Law of the jungle. Winning is a simple matter of the survival of the fittest. For every winner there must be a loser. If you have money and power, you can win. If you don't, forget it. The concepts of winning and serving are incompatible. How can you win and lend a helping hand at the same time? You've got to do it to others before they do it to you.

Sour grapes. All this talk about winning is a waste of time. Slogans like "Winning isn't everything; it's the only thing" are juvenile locker room mania. If you do get to the top, it takes too much time and effort. And once you're there, it's not only lonely but it's precarious as well. Someone younger, stronger, faster, better looking, is just itching to bring you down.

Survivalist. Winning is just getting through the week without getting killed. You earn your money, take what's left after Uncle Sam and the bill collectors get through with you, and try to find a little pleasure on the weekends. Winning is simply surviving in this fouled-up world and escaping the rat race when you can.

All of the above attitudes are reflections of what I believe is the dominant view of winning and success that influences our culture. This philosophy says power is god and no-holds-barred competition and comparison are his prophets. This extremely popular view of success can be labeled simply *win-lose.* To the victors belong the spoils, not to mention the headlines, the prestige, and a bottom line that is always written in basic, profit-beautiful black.

The win-lose approach feeds on the concept of invidious comparison. "Where's the Beef?" the slick commercials parrot, comparing one supposedly superior fast-food burger with another inferior one. "Ours is ninety-eight percent real beef. Theirs is laced with additives and shrinks under the broiler, until it disappears inside the bun. Ours is Number One."

Is Competition the Real Culprit?

Am I saying it is inherently wrong for one burger chain or rent-a-car franchise or any business to compete with another? Hardly. Competition provides the soil in which free enterprise and democracy can take root. We all know what happens when a company or group has no competition. Seldom does lack of competition result in reasonable prices or good service. Competition in itself is not the culprit. No, the real culprits are the insatiable drives for status and power that we find deep within all of us.

Let's face it. The idea of being Number One is attractive. So is the idea of success. There is nothing inherently wrong with desiring success. Given a choice, naturally all of us would rather succeed than fail. In defense of the success books (my own included), they contain a great deal of common sense and practical realism that will help anyone take more responsibility for his own actions. Those of us who seek to tell people how to succeed believe there is a lot to be said for taking charge of your life and making your own decisions, instead of just floating with the tide and feeling like a victim, or at best a semi-interested spectator.

Unfortunately, the positive side of winning is matched by a dark side. Like Luke Skywalker we want "the force to be with us," but it is all too easy to sell out to the "dark side of the force" in order to succeed.

We can see the evidence all around us. In our status-oriented culture, winning at the expense of others is more important than winning by sharing with and caring for others. Healthy competition to ensure quality in a free market has given way to "knocking the other guy" in order to look good. This trend toward "dirty politics" among peers and organizations, and our obsession with success at any price, have resulted in the distortion of our basic values. We have become so addicted to immediate sensual gratification that we live in constant anxiety that can be relieved only by some successful accomplishment, adornment, or elixir. In our culture, pleasure has not only come to mean the absence of pain; pleasure has become one of our major national pastimes. And there is no question that winning and winners are a big part of our pleasure seeking. Everybody loves a winner, envies a winner, wants to be a winner. Nobody crowds around the loser's locker room. There is only one Miss America, one Super Bowl champion, and one winning candidate. The runners-up and also-rans are forgotten immediately.

The Problem With One-Way Winning

Winning by comparison, by domination, arrogance, or aggression is one-way winning. It's an "I win, you lose" philosophy.

"For every winner, there's a loser."

"I got mine, too bad you didn't get yours."

"Do it to others before they do it to you."

"You've got to be Number One. Nobody's going to take care of you in this life but *you*, so you've got to get down, push-shove-grit-and-groan your way to the top."

Today's "winning warp" has caused me to see that like any good thing, winning can become twisted and perverted. I have decided it is time for someone who deals in helping people succeed and win to speak out against the all-too-many success formulas built around the win-lose concept. I fervently believe in seeking success and being a winner, but *how I go about it* is critical. If I concentrate on "winning by intimidation," and "looking out for Number One," it is all too easy to develop a narcissistic, self-indulgent attitude. Perhaps the key spokesman for this kind of win-lose approach is Robert J. Ringer, the best-selling author of *Winning by Intimidation* and *Looking Out for Number One*.

How to Look Out for Number One

In 1973 Robert J. Ringer hit the best-seller list with *Winning by Intimidation*. Four years later he followed up with an even bigger blockbuster entitled *Looking Out for Number One*. The book's jacket cites Ringer's "emergence as the 'people's philosopher of the 70's,' " a title he earned by discarding "irrational customs and traditions" to guide his readers on "the most exciting and rewarding journey of their lives."

As he looks out for Number One, Robert Ringer abhors the Absolute Moralists who relentlessly talk about deciding what is right for everyone else. Ringer also tries to disassociate himself from the hedonists who pursue pleasure for pleasure's sake. According to Ringer, "Man's primary moral duty lies in the pursuit of pleasure so long as he does not forcibly interfere with the rights of others."[1] Ringer believes all of us act in our own self-interest all the time, so why be so hush-hush about it?[2] Rational selfishness, says Ringer, is okay. When you are rationally selfish, you don't forcibly interfere in the rights and lives of others. Irrational selfishness is the culprit you must watch out for. And who are the irrationally selfish? The Absolute Moralists, of course, who selfishly interfere in your life by encouraging and even coercing you to do what they think is right.[3]

While he encourages his readers to do what *he* thinks is right, Ringer pursues his argument further by pointing out that the dictionary's definition of *selfishness* "distorts" the issue. He quotes one dictionary that defines selfishness as "caring only or chiefly for oneself; regarding one's own interest chiefly or solely." Ringer believes that *solely* regarding and *chiefly* regarding your own interests are two different things. He emphasizes that we always act selfishly because it's an automatic reflex. We really have no choice. The issue is whether we will be rational or irrational in our selfishness.

If we are rationally selfish, we will *chiefly* regard our own interests, but not *solely*. Simple logic tells Ringer that we must regard the interests of others at least some of the time in order to gain our objectives. The rationally selfish person, says Ringer, is a very giving person because he understands the importance of "value for value relationships." In other words, if we do give something to others, we expect something back. Ringer fears gifts given by so-called unselfish folk, because he believes they have hidden price tags and an unspoken accounts-payable due date.[4]

As you read Ringer's arguments you have to admit they contain a certain amount of truth. For example, "quid pro quo"—something for something—is a cornerstone of economics. To not forcibly interfere with the rights of others is also a good idea (even if it might cause Ringer chagrin to realize he has stated a "moral absolute"). And acting selfishly *is* an automatic reflex. In fact we are born with it. The question is whether or not it is desirable to develop such a reflex or try to curb it. If I go about being rationally selfish (meaning I pursue pleasure without forcibly interfering with the rights of others), I operate from a foundation that says I am most important, and while I don't want to hurt anyone, I am not primarily concerned with helping anyone, either. There is also the knotty problem of pursuing my pleasures and unknowingly interfering with the rights of others because I am too busy concentrating on me, myself, and mine.

As for differentiating between "chiefly" or "solely" regarding one's own interests, I believe Ringer is playing word games. According to Ringer it is okay to *chiefly* regard your own interests. This is rational selfishness and is quite acceptable. But to *solely* regard my own interests is a no-no. That would be irrational. Again, Ringer's logic is clear. He realizes that acting selfishly all the time would be too easy to spot. People would soon turn on you and refuse to cooperate in helping you pursue your own pleasures. To act selfishly all the time is not a value-for-value approach. No one would play your game.

But as he "chiefly pursues his own interests," Ringer can be far more subtle. Again, he is operating from the stance that says he is most important. Others are not there to be served or helped. *They are to be used, because his pleasure is the primary consideration.* Remember that pursuit of pleasure is, in Ringer's words, "man's primary moral duty," just as long as he is rational about it.

But who is to say what is rational? How can Ringer always know when he is being rational or irrational as he looks out for Number One? And when does *chiefly* pursuing his own interests drift over the line into *solely* pursuing his own interests because he wants to win? Ringer is a major spokesman for the win-lose philosophy. He works from a foundation that demands he must win (obtain pleasure) and *his interests always come first.* Ringer's position forces him to live while wearing blinders equipped with mirrors. All he really sees is himself, because pleasure is the be-all and end-all of life.

What Happens When Win-Lose Goes to Seed?

Bookstores are loaded with other authors who join Ringer on the win-lose side of the scale. You can find just about anything from how to get power and mastery over people to how to live (yes, even "dress") for success while you get what you want, have it all, and succeed at any price.[5] And the price is high when these win-lose philosophies of success get out of hand. It is not hard to see that it is only a short step from looking out for Number One and succeeding by undermining others to narcissism and self-indulgence. Neither state keeps you in the winner's circle in the long run. Narcissus, you may recall, was the mythical character who pined away and finally died as he stared self-lovingly at his own image reflected in a clear pool of water.

In his insightful book *Me: The Narcissistic American,* Dr. Aaron Stern pointedly observes that we are not born with the desire to love others. A baby is a complete narcissist, interested in only his own needs. As the baby grows up he develops the capacity to love his parents, then others. Stern writes:

> Narcissism and the capacity to love are directly related to each other. As one element increases, inevitably the other must decrease. The more narcissistic one is, the less he can love and vice versa. But no human being is absolutely capable of loving others. Narcissistic drives are always getting in the way. One can only love in relative terms.

The struggle to prevent our narcissitic selves from overwhelming our caring selves is an enduring one. It is man's fate. It begins at birth and continues to the moment of his death. In the best of circumstances it is an inherent human weakness that is always difficult to overcome.[6]

It is chillingly ironic that books like Ringer's, which are really not so subtly disguised treatises on how to become a narcissist, are *bestsellers*. Hundreds of thousands buy these books; how many buy the philosophy? As a "teacher of how to be successful," I believe success enriches our lives and contributes to our sense of worth. Success is not the problem, per se; *it is what success can do to us*. The real problem is the insatiable appetite for power that it generates. Stern, a psychoanalyst who has taught at Yale, Columbia, and UCLA, believes "Narcissism breeds power, and power breeds narcissism. Each exists because of the other and both serve to make each other grow."[7] But to seek, or even hold, power is a losing game. "Power always corrupts. Power is an interest in exercising control over others."[8]

Like the fleeting glimpse of a monarch butterfly, power is always on the verge of disappearing. The "king of the mountain" is like Humpty Dumpty, precariously perched for the great fall. The more power gained for self-gratification, the greater the fear of losing it. Power is like drinking sea water. The more you consume, the thirstier you get.

Power and sharing are polarized concepts. Sharing exposes us to considering the needs of others, thus subordinating some of our own desires for gratification. The power habit is fueled by status symbols and "perks" that range from cars, special lunchrooms, parking spaces, and office suites to designer jeans, monogrammed shirts, stadium box seats, and chains of gold dangling from everywhere.

Win-Lose Gets You Hooked on Power

Power, says Stern, is like any other narcissistic behavior; it becomes addictive. As we move up the ladder of success, we want increased dosages. "Pretty soon it's the only way to go. It's more than a kick; it becomes a way of life. We're hooked."[9]

The thirst and drive for power are everywhere, but they are

especially present in the corporate and business world. Until recently the classic corporation approach to success was patterned after the win-lose model. And win-lose *can* get results, at least for the short haul. Proof of this was the tenure of Harold Geneen, who took over International Telephone and Telegraph when it was going nowhere slowly. He set up a competitive system of management that stressed decentralization of ITT into many divisions that could check on and compete with one another according to "the unshakeable facts."

A major feature of Geneen's system was his monthly review of all the company's divisions, which was conducted around a giant conference table equipped with microphones and capable of seating 150 people. Division managers had to make their reports and be subject to the keenest and most ruthless interrogation, which was designed to root out any signs of uncertainty and weakness. Equipped with an infallible memory, Geneen often led in the questioning and would tear a weak presentation to shreds. More than one manager was reduced to tears under the grueling pressure.

For many years the win-lose management-by-stress approach paid off. To his credit, ITT climbed to the summit of success mountain during Geneen's tenure. According to Robert Sobel in *The Rise and Fall of the Conglomerate Kings* (Stein and Day, 1984), Geneen was the master of a certain bottom-line strategy of the sixties and seventies that saw corporate management as a strategy of balance-sheet buying and selling. Geneen was praised and the object of case studies at the Harvard Business School.

As long as Geneen was present to drive his win-lose philosophy, it worked, though it put managers under constant stress and intimidation. His method also led to riskier and sometimes stressful business as managers strived not to be losers. When Geneen left ITT, it was a different story. The press focused more on management blunders than successes. The public read stories of overseas bribery—during Geneen's reign—by ITT officials trying to survive within the Geneen system.[10]

It took Geneen's replacement, Rand V. Araskog, years to heal the internal wounds and public image of the conglomerate. Here's what *New York Times* reporter Leslie Wayne said in a long article on ITT in the Sunday paper five years after Geneen's departure:

The lanky Mr. Araskog is widely described as a mild-mannered man . . . in contrast to Mr. Geneen, who had the reputation of an overbearing autocrat who ruled through intimidation. Mr. Araskog has gone a long way toward reshaping the culture of a global corporation that carried the personal imprint of Mr. Geneen, for good or bad.

To the relief of many employees, Mr. Araskog has done away with such Geneen trademarks as the huge corporate meetings in which employees were dressed down in front of the group. Mr. Araskog has also reorganized ITT's hundreds of businesses into four main divisions—corporations in their own right—and has decentralized decision making and pushed it down into the operating level. He has made ITT efficient, if a little duller.

"Instead of a razzmatazz conglomerate doing a deal a minute and having the financial people pirouetting, the atmosphere of ITT is one of a tighter, more traditional business organization," said Mr. Fernandez [Brian R. Fernandez, an analyst with Nomura Securities]. "It's less based on star magnetism and more on back to basics. To the outside, the culture used to be one of working eighteen hours a day and having an answer to every question. It almost appeared as if internal performance was as important, if not more important, than business achievement."[11]

Authors Terrence Deal and Allan Kennedy, who chronicle Geneen's win-lose regime at ITT in *Corporate Cultures*, sum up by saying:

Managers like Geneen are guided by an *ethic of competition*, of winning the game. Heroes, by contrast, are driven by an *ethic of creation*. They inspire employees by distributing a sense of responsibility throughout the organization. Everybody performs with tangible goals in sight. There is more tolerance for risk taking, thus greater innovation; more acceptance of the value of long-term success, thus greater persistence; more personal responsibility for how the company performs—thus a work force that identifies personal achievement with the success of its firm.[12]

The Win-Lose World Is Obsolete

Are the heroes described by Deal and Kennedy a figment of their idealism? Are there any corporations and managers today who are driven more by the "ethic of creation" rather than the "ethic of competition" that banks everything on winning the game? During the past seven years, I have crisscrossed the land dozens of times, addressing executives and managers in over half the Fortune 500 companies in the nation. I have also talked with many of their spouses and children. Everywhere I go I have heard growing protests against the pressures and stress of living in the win-lose philosophy. In so many words executives are saying: "I'm tired of the stockholders and the bottom line. I know we have to make a profit, but must profit always come ahead of people?"

And corporate wives are saying: "Must we keep putting pressure on our kids to do the best all the time? I know it's a competitive world, but when do we let our children—and ourselves—relax?"

I see a painful metamorphosis taking place in society that is every bit as dramatic as the magic transformation of the caterpillar into the butterfly. The very nature of winning is in transition. Our former basis for defining winning, according to external standards set by a hedonistic, egocentric, highly impressionable society, is being transformed. The new view of winning is based on *internal* standards which, while differing for each individual, are consistent in that they take into account moral and spiritual values and principles that affect all of humankind and the natural world.

In the next chapter I'll describe what I believe to be the only viable alternative to the win-lose syndrome. *Success must become a two-way street.* The win-win philosophy—what I have come to call the Double Win—is the only approach that can endure.

An Idea Long Overdue

You've heard it so many times it's become a cliché: "It's an idea whose time has come." When I talk about the Double Win, I like to describe it as "an idea that is long overdue."

Just What Is the Double Win?

A brief and simple definition of the Double Win is:

"If I help you win, I win, too."

"Sounds like a riddle to me," I've heard people say. So, I go on to explain that the real winners in life get what they want by helping others get what they want. Independence is replaced by interdependence. We must face the inescapable fact that we, as individuals, are vital but single organs of a larger body of human beings that make up the world.

There are too many people, too few resources, and too delicate a balance between nature and technology to produce winners in isolation today. As individuals we cannot succeed or even survive for long anymore without the others.[1]

Granted, this is not an easy message to sell to a culture that has been nursed, weaned, and nurtured on the win-lose concept. There is probably no more powerful salesman of the win-lose approach than the televising of sporting events. Throughout the year, millions watch highly overpaid gifted athletes do their thing on the diamond, gridiron, and hardwood, not to mention various courts, tracks, and courses. Add the televising of amateur athletics and there is a literal twenty-four-hour barrage of sports available.

And always the message from the wide world of sports is the same: the thrill of victory and the agony of defeat. Could we call a tie a Double Win? Certainly not, and besides, ties are practically ruled out by overtimes, play-offs, sudden deaths, and two-point conversions. Woe to the coach who plays for a tie when he can go for a field goal or touchdown to win it all.

Let's Try, "Be All You Can Be!"

So what am I suggesting? That we abolish sports and as many other forms of win-lose competition as possible? As I mentioned in chapter 1, competition is not the problem. Competition—be it in the marketplace, polling place, or playing place—sharpens skills, exposes poor and shoddy efforts, stands guard against gorging and greed, and motivates us to be the best we can be. But what is missing in today's win-lose society is a spirit of cooperation and creativity, a feeling that it is more important to help everyone develop his or her potential as a human being rather than simply get on the scoreboard and add another win to the victory column.

I love athletics as much as the next person, probably more so than many who will read this book. Since 1980, I have served as Chairman of Psychology on the U.S. Olympic Committee Sports Medicine Council. Our job on the council was to enhance the performance of our Olympic athletes, and we spent long hours working with skiers, skaters, sprinters, jumpers, leapers, and throwers of all kinds.

In the words of a U.S. Army commercial, we tried to help our Olympic performers "be all that they could be." If they won the Gold, great! If they finished well back in a pack of thirty or forty, also great, as long as they gave it all they had, and could say they had reached down deep for as much excellence as they had in them. A brief look at history shows the Olympic Games were founded on the "be all you can be" principle, not "get all the Gold you can."

The Greeks Had a Better Idea

The first Olympiad was held in 776 B.C., the first accurately attested date in Greek history. The first historical personalities we know of as "winners" were the athletes who won victories in these games.

Recognizing the unity of spirit, nature, body, and mind, the Greeks created the Olympic Games in celebration of the harmony of the cosmos. They saw the Games as much more than mere athletic competition. Their Olympic athletes were trained by coaches, scholars, physicians, and clergy, not only in sports but also in religion, the arts, philosophy, politics, and music. The athletic games were only one form of Olympic competition; there were also musical, theatrical, and artistic events for the public's enjoyment and for the participants' means of expressing individual and team excellence.

The ancient Olympics flourished until Rome conquered Greece in 146 B.C. Roman indifference and corruption eventually led to the abolishment of the Games in 393 A.D. When Baron Pierre de Coubertin conceived the idea of reviving the Olympics in Athens in 1896, he was inspired by the original principles that had fostered the Games in the first place:

- the value of whole person in spirit, body, and mind
- the belief in individual freedom and merit
- a consciousness of our individual and collective responsibilities to each other
- an acceptance of our democratic right to participate in public affairs

Many believe this idea of peace, love, and brotherhood throughout the world to be a Pollyanna vision seen through rose-colored glasses. Nonetheless, the original idea of winning behind the Olympic Games was that there is a place and time where the boundaries dividing people are forgotten; where heritage, language, race, and religious belief raise no barriers between individuals; where social order of birth, national power, or material wealth are of no account; where individuals, stripped of their labels, compete with their neighbors peacefully and honorably, solely to be the best they can be. The hope was that this Olympic spirit could carry over to inspire the whole world, not just for a few days of an Olympiad every four years but every day of every year. The early Olympians sought a harmony built upon a twofold goal: develop individual ability and give it proper merit and recognition while never forgetting the collective responsibility they had to one another.[2]

God-Made Men or Man-Made Gods?

But somewhere along the way, the idea of winning in harmony got warped. It probably began going astray with the ancient Greeks themselves, who began to place too much emphasis on the fame associated with victory, and the idea of man-made gods, rather than God-made men. The hedonistic Romans certainly added to the distortion. Our image of a Roman athletic contest is that of a gladiator in the Coliseum, standing victoriously with one foot on a fallen adversary, callously asking the spectators for a thumbs-up or thumbs-down sentence for the vanquished. Here winning wasn't everything—it was the only thing. Competition was demeaned by the violence and vulgarity of the contest.

Today the Olympic spirit is marred by overemphasis on "going for the Gold." The Olympics have become a political football that has been fumbled every four years of late, first by the United States and then by the Russians. Though the future of the Games may be cloudy, the commercial impact of gold medals still glitters brightly. The great new American success story now envisions the hero or heroine practicing for years, winning the Gold in a dazzling exhibition of flawless skill, and then skating into the sunset with a fat contract from the Ice Capades, a sporting-goods company, or a television network.

And why not? Didn't the gold-medal winners earn it? You have to get all you can while you can. Climb to the top of the heap. Nobody looks out for you but yourself. Hear those footsteps? Plenty of competitors are right on your tail, hoping to knock you off. Them that has, should be sure that their agents get them more. It's the American way.

Or is it?

Can Winning Buy Happiness?

I am thoroughly convinced that we must reassess what we mean when we talk about winning. I believe you don't have to knock other people down to win. Victory is not gained only at someone's expense, and every victory does not result in a defeat. Winning is taking the talent or potential you were born with, and have since developed, and using it fully toward a goal or purpose that makes you happy and simultaneously serves other people. In fact, it's the serving that's more important, because happiness is not a goal in itself.

Happiness is the experience of having lived a life that you feel is worthwhile. Happiness, to me, is the natural experience of winning your own self-respect, as well as the respect of others.

Happiness should not be confused with indulgence, escapism, or hedonistic pleasure-seeking. You can't smoke, inhale, or snort happiness. You can't buy it, drive it, fly it, swallow it, inject it, or travel to it. Happiness is the journey, not the destination. Elusive as a butterfly, happiness comes only to those who feel it without chasing it, and who can give it away *without expecting a payoff.*

Beyond Quid Pro Quo

Earlier in my search for what makes a person a successful winner, I was attracted to the notion that if I give you what you want and you give me what I need, we have exchanged value and both of us win. It is a logical idea, a practical idea—but a win-lose idea. Robert Ringer pushes it to its outer limits in *Looking Out for Number One.* Ringer, you will recall, teaches that the rationally selfish person is very giving because he understands the importance of value-for-value relationships. Ringer lives by this credo to the extent that he cannot believe someone would give him a gift strictly for the pleasure of giving it. For Ringer, all gifts have price tags. All people should live by the motto "quid pro quo"—I give you something, I get something in return.

But in my travels and my own relationships, I kept encountering winning individuals who seemed quite willing to pass on some of their "winnings" to others, yet they apparently suffered no loss. In fact, they seemed to gain from the experience.

I have concluded that "passing on your wins" is more important than merely making a mutual exchange of value. The key that turns the happiness lock is appreciating the value of my own wins (some of my own immediate pleasure), but even then I gain the added satisfaction of sharing with another.

Double Winning is winning by shared values. Life challenges us to seek the Double Win at all levels: personal, family, social, and corporate. The Double Win is not a new idea. It has been around for centuries in the teachings of Jesus of Nazareth. It has revolutionized companies and corporations throughout past decades. In the workplace, if employees see themselves as competent, valued, and important to the employer, regardless of their status in the hierarchy, they tend to respond with higher quality of goods and services provided to the customers, which results in higher profits for stockholders. Everybody wins!

It has happened and continues to happen in corporations like IBM, General Electric, National Cash Register, and 3M. The same kind of Double Win nurturing is going on throughout Japanese industry. In fact, so successful have the Japanese become in the world marketplace with their tender-loving-care approach to employees that their methods are envied and studied by business leaders around the world.

Corporate Cultures and the Double Win

According to Terrence Deal and Allan Kennedy, authors of *Corporate Cultures*, every company has a "culture" of some kind, which can be informally defined as "the way we do things around here."[3] Companies with strong cultures usually have clearly focused values that are transmitted to all employees. In a six-month study of almost eighty firms, Deal and Kennedy found eighteen that had what they call qualitative beliefs, which are often expressed in company slogans like "IBM means service" and General Electric's "Progress is our most important product."[4]

All of these strong culture organizations were consistently high performers. What goes into making a strong culture besides developing slogans? In example after example, Deal and Kennedy describe companies where the Double Win ("I help you win and I win, too") is practiced in one way or another.

"It Takes Two to Tandem"

One stellar illustration is Tandem Computer, one of the new high-tech firms springing up in the Silicon Valley, just south of San Francisco. Tandem was founded by four former employees of Hewlett-Packard (another strong culture corporation just down the road). Tandem's product is an ingenious method for linking two computers in one mainframe to ensure available computer power at all times. If one computer breaks down, the other is a backup. One of Tandem's managers describes the company this way:

> "Tandem is saying something about the product and people work-ing together. Everything here works together. People with people; product with product; even processor with processor, within the product. Everything works together to keep us where we are."[5]

And from the rank and file at Tandem come comments like these:

> "I feel like putting a lot of time in. There is a real kind of loyalty here. We are all working in this together—working a process to-gether. I'm not a workaholic—it's just the place. I love the place."

> "I don't want anything in the world that would hurt Tandem. I feel totally divorced from my old company, not Tandem."[6]

At Tandem, which has grown at a rate of 25 percent *per quarter* (annual revenues 100 million), management philosophy em-phasizes the importance of people. Along with its people, creative action and fun are called Tandem's greatest resources. The philoso-phy is present everywhere, worn on employee tee shirts or posted on bulletin boards. Two samples:

> "It takes two to Tandem."
> "Tandemize it—means make it work."[7]

To many caught in the typical win-lose web of corporate intrigue and bureaucratic red tape, Tandem sounds like at least a suburb of heaven. There is no formal organizational chart, few meetings and memos, and flexible working hours. There are no name tags and Tandem president Jim Treybig parks in an unreserved space like everyone else. Treybig, who is viewed by his employees as a hero, has an open-door policy, as do his managers and vice-presidents. The goal at Tandem is to have everyone—from janitor to president—communicate and feel that he is valued and important.

At Tandem, all employees enjoy the company golf course, exercise room, and swimming pool. Every Friday afternoon is company party time and everyone attends, not simply to wind down from the busy week but to informally communicate and brainstorm. In addition, there are company-wide celebrations on important holidays, another means of creating a feeling of oneness. The net result is that Tandem employees feel special and they in turn feel the company and its product are special. Typical comment:

> "My goals follow the company's. It's the company and I. I think that's pretty true of everyone. We all want to see it work. My job is important, and if I don't do it, Tandem doesn't make a buck."[8]

Can Camelot Last at Tandem?

Obviously there is a little more going on at Tandem Computer than a simple quid pro quo approach in which management does nice things for the employees in the hope that employees will reciprocate with loyal efficiency. There is a love and concern for people and product that is light-years away from the calculating cynicism of lookers-out-for-Number-One like Ringer and his counterparts. Tandem management shares its wins with its people but really gives up nothing. Instead, everyone gains; everyone wins.

Will Tandem's Camelot last? Authors Deal and Kennedy observe that in a company this new only time will tell. But they believe Tandem is off to an excellent start in evolving the same kind of strong culture that has been evident for decades in such giants as IBM and GE.[9]

Keep in mind, however, that companies with strong cultures are not always as freewheeling and easygoing in managerial style as Jim Treybig at Tandem. Tom Watson, who guided IBM to the very top of American industry, was a hard-driving type who "could be a benevolent boss, but even IBMers who worshiped him never considered Watson a friend or, given his obsessiveness, a very pleasant person to be around."[10] Nonetheless, Watson clearly grasped the principles of the Double Win when he instituted a passion for service to the customer. At IBM the promising newcomers are assigned to spend a year as "assistant" to senior managers. One of their chief tasks is answering customer complaint letters. "A dubious reward for early managerial promise? Indeed not. This seemingly ho-hum function ensures an increased sensitivity on their part to the importance that IBM attaches to customer service."[11]

To repeat, a company with a strong culture (sense of how we do things around here) will tend to practice more of the win-win philosophy than the win-lose. As Deal and Kennedy point out: "A strong culture enables people to feel better about what they do, so they are more likely to work harder."[12]

Double Winner Charles Steinmetz

Another strong culture builder and practitioner of the Double Win was Charles Steinmetz, a crippled Austrian immigrant who worked in Thomas Edison's lab and later became Chief Engineer of General Electric. In Steinmetz's dwarflike body resided the mind of a genius. He was responsible for dozens of inventions, including alternating electrical current. Still revered today at GE as a legendary figure, Steinmetz had a Double Win heart to match his intellect. When a young engineer joined GE, Steinmetz would invite him to stay at his home for the weekend, simply to get to know and understand him as a person. "Once he adopted one of GE's leading engineers as his own son—and the man's whole family. They all moved into Steinmetz's house and lived with him for twenty years."[13]

Today, GE is known for its supportive climate that encourages— even demands—that people treat each other fairly. Again, here is a simple illustration of the Double Win. It is hard to see a strong corporate culture like GE's advocating that employees be greedy or that they practice honesty and loyalty only when it seems expedient.

Cynics may shrug and still maintain that companies like Tandem and GE are simply practicing "smart business," but the differences between win-lose and win-win are more than subtle. Double Winners create other winners without exploiting them. Those who practice the win-lose way of life ultimately must exploit others because others exist to be made use of in one way or another.

The win-lose attitude is, "I'm only really concerned with me—first and last. I may share with you somewhere in between, but only because I have the bottom line clearly in my sights."

The win-win attitude says: "I live every moment, enjoying the most, relating as much, doing as much, and giving as much as I possibly can. I enjoy the Double Win because it ensures victories for me *and* others. I don't worry about the bottom line because, if I give life all I've got, the bottom line takes care of itself."

The Cynics Say, "No Way!"

The win-win attitude sounds good—even noble and altruistic—but can it work? Can anyone actually live this unselfishly? There are plenty of cynics and skeptics who say, "No way!" For example, Robert Ringer, articulate expert in the art of taking care of Number One, believes that nobody can live by the win-win rules because everybody is basically selfish. According to Ringer, Mahatma Gandhi acted selfishly when he lived a life of total sacrifice to gain freedom for his nation of India. He believes Gandhi was like any other human being who had to choose from alternatives available at the time. Ringer writes: "If he acted in the hope of making millions of his countrymen happy, then that was the method he chose to seek his own happiness. It's only the means people choose to achieve their happiness that differ."[14]

Ringer believes that martyrs like Gandhi ". . . are selfish people the same as you and me—but with insatiable egos." Ringer believes that acts of sacrifice, whether at Gandhi's level or in simple everyday acts with your family and friends, are all done for selfish reasons. You may sacrifice for your children, your spouse, your parents, your boss, but "none of these examples, of course, really involves sacrifice at all. What is involved, at its highest level, is rational selfishness—acting on the belief that the good you hope to receive in return will be worth the time, effort and/or money you extend in doing something for the other person."[15]

Ringer has little use for philanthropists or altruistic acts. He warns, "Be especially wary of those who actually believe they're altruistic, for they are the most vain and dangerous of all people."[16]

Ringer, therefore, would not be impressed by the charity volunteer who, instead of enjoying reading to the blind in pleasant, clean surroundings, chooses to go to the worst part of town to work in a soup kichen serving drunken, diseased, and depressed old men. It would be the choice that made her happiest. The same holds true for the person who could write a nice-size check for charity, but instead signs on as an orderly at a hospital where he will be exposed to somber sights, sounds, and smells, not to mention dread disease.

Let us be willing to admit that Ringer has a point. There *are* people who thrive on the dangerous, the hard, the sacrificial act. To do less would be dull, boring, unfulfilling. The tougher it is, the more pleasure they receive. But no one, not even Ringer, is claiming that you have to suffer or face hardship to validate a kindly or unselfish act.

Ringer believes there is no such thing as an unselfish act; there are only acts of rational selfishness that we all do with a quid pro quo, value-for-value motive. But in watching the Double Win at work in my own life, as well as the lives of others, I have learned that you can give value without giving away anything. When you are motivated by the Double Win philosophy, you are able to keep the full value of your own wins and impart new value to others.

This new value is created out of the very act of giving. This new value does not exist until it is given away to the other person. It is as though, upon reaching out my hand to you, something new is created. I could not have it, I could not keep it, I could not use it. But at that very moment, I get the rich return of having given it to you. I may have given something away, but I have given up nothing. I have created the Double Win.

Double Win at Sarajevo

And just how does all this work? Millions saw it in action at the 1984 Olympic Games at Sarajevo, Yugoslavia. The weather was anything but ideal for the men's slalom competition. It was cold and bleak on Bjelasnica Mountain. A biting wind tore through the spectators, athletes, and officials. It had been an unpredictable week. People won who were least expected to, while the heralded favorites finished as unlikely also-rans. The usual cheerfulness and exuberance were strangely missing.

The Mahre twins, Steve and Phil, seemed quiet and somber—after all, this was to be their last hurrah, their last battle with the world's finest. The media, and thus the millions back home, began to wonder if they'd lost the winning edge. Maybe they had won *too* frequently. We heard them say that winning a gold medal was no big thing after winning the World Cup. The Olympic flame within them seemed to be slowly flickering out. Their performance in the Giant Slalom had been mediocre, and nothing better was expected on this final day of ski competition in 1984's Olympic Winter Games.

Phil Mahre's number came up first. He "wasn't real pleased" with his first run, but the second time down he described it as a "good clean run . . . concentrated, took a little more risk." His combined time was 1 minute, 39:41 seconds, good enough to put him in first place for the moment. Still waiting at the top for his second run was Steve Mahre, whose time on his first effort left him with an excellent shot at the gold. Born only minutes apart and always intense competitors, the Mahre twins were in their own private shoot-out for Olympic glory!

The "natural" thing for Phil to do at that point was to wait, saying nothing, hoping his time would stand up. Instead he grabbed a walkie-talkie and began radioing advice to Steve, who was still waiting at the top of the icy slope. Phil urged Steve to "look ahead," and "ski a straight course" but he warned that "the bottom was slick."

Down came Steve, who by his own admission made at least three mistakes that cost him valuable time. In addition, his skis got locked and he couldn't turn left properly on part of the run. With all that he still finished only .21 seconds behind his brother, good enough for a silver medal.

Steve's comment after he learned he had missed the gold by a fraction was, "You have to put two runs together. Phil did that today. No one else did."

What about the walkie-talkie message? Steve said: "Phil has gold in his hand and he's telling me, 'Okay, you gotta do this to beat me.' "

Watching the medal ceremony, as two American flags climbed

into the Sarajevo sky, spectators with *true* vision saw gold medals around both brothers' necks. From the stage of a steep and icy slalom run in Yugoslavia, the Mahre twins showed the world just what the Double Win is.

By getting on that walkie-talkie, Phil had said in so many words to his brother, "If I help you win, I win, too. You may win today, and I tomorrow, but I'm going to give you all my best, because that's what gives me the gold medal *within.*"

And then, as if to place winning in its ultimate perspective, Phil answered the expected question ("How do you feel after winning the Gold?") with this reply: "I was never in the sport to win one cent. I was here to compete. I was here to perform to my abilities. I was in the sport because I loved it, and I love it to this day."[17]

Phil and Steve were able to hang up their competitive skis shortly after Sarajevo, but they will always know what true winning is:

> I *do* my best, and I *give* my best. I help my fellow man "down the hill" (or "up the hill" as the case may be), all the while keeping my values in proper perspective. If I can help you win, I share in the victory. We *both* win. Success is a two-way street.

LOSERS SAY	WINNERS SAY	DOUBLE WINNERS SAY
"There is no way I can win."	"I'll do everything I can to win."	"If you win, I win, too."

3

Profile of a Double Winner

When the Mahre twins skied to that Double Win at Sarajevo, they were models for multitudes across the world who seek to live with the attitude "If I help you win, I win, too."

Throughout this book, I will be telling Double Win stories from a file I've built over the years. But I know some of the best win-win examples will never be reported because:

- the winners are not seeking publicity for their acts
- good news is not the favorite grist of the news-media mill
- many Double Wins are small, everyday encounters, affecting the lives of only a few people, even though that effect may be profound

By design, several of my Double Win illustrations come from the world of sports, professional and amateur. If you are not a sports buff, I apologize for possibly overdoing the athletic side. Regardless of our interest or lack of same in athletics, however, the world of sports offers a meticulously media-monitored microcosm of all our lives as we strive to cope with the daily battle.

I've come to view life as a marvelous game, with no substitutions, no time-outs, and a running clock. During the first two quarters (when I was younger), I used to think of life as a practice scrimmage, a preparation for the real thing. But during halftime (mid-life), it has dawned on me that there are only four quarters of effort in this body, although my soul will go on to another realm. The game is *real* and *every day* is the Super Bowl. As John Wayne said to his young cowhands in the film *Cowboys*, "We're burnin' daylight!"

Four Kinds of People Come to Life's Big Game

I also realized that while the game we call life is going on, non-stop, four kinds of people are in the stadium.

1. *The spectators* are the vast majority who watch life happen from the stands. They seem to avoid the main arena for fear of being rejected or ridiculed, hurt or defeated. They prefer not to make waves or get involved, and would rather watch it all happen on television. It's not really losing they fear the most. It's quite comfortable to lose and rationalize it by saying: "It's not meant to be; it's not my fault; and besides, who can make it nowadays with the inflationary cycle, the high deficit, and the constant threat of 'the nuclear day after'?"

No, it's not losing they fear solely—it's also the possibility of winning. After all, winning carries the burden of responsibility to set a good example, to step out in the open to be ridiculed and tested by your peers. That's too much of an effort for most people, so they choose to sit back and watch others perform.

2. *The losers* make up the next group. By losers, I do not mean the people who are losing due to catastrophe, bad breaks, illness, or other adversity. By losers, I do not refer to the millions of hungry, destitute people throughout the world. Losers are not people who are born with no head start in a ghetto that can provide only the most meager education.

By "losers," I mean people who *choose to lose.* They never see themselves winning because they'd rather look like, dress like, have fun like, earn like, have a house like, or be like somebody else. You can always spot losers by the way they envy and criticize others. Because misery loves company, losers are adept at putting themselves and other people down.

3. *One-way winners* are the followers of the win-lose philosophy discussed in chapters 1 and 2. One-way winners define *victory* as the domination and defeat of others. They may talk about "negotiating value for value" and other "quid pro quos," but their only real feelings of responsibility are to themselves. Ultimately, for them, there is winning or there is nothing.

People who practice the single win travel a one-way street. They usually become arrogant, because they can't help comparing themselves with others. In one way or another, they are always saying, "I built my monument to my progress. Come see what I built." They become hardened and cold—closed to new opportunities and ideas. Their hardness can range from intellectual cynicism to indifference and apathy. It can include prejudice and aloofness, and when it goes totally to seed, vulgarity and rudeness.

4. *The Double Winners* are a smaller but growing group that understands the path toward authentic, continual, lifelong winning: Success is a two-way street. This path is one's own pursuit of individual excellence, which involves neither luck, astrological forecasts, or being beautiful, thin, powerful, and rich. The Double Win is *giving* and *getting* in an atmosphere of love, cooperation, social concern, and responsibility.

We are all aware that to win *over* others we must have determination, goals, dogged persistence, and incurable optimism that we will prevail, in spite of the odds. There have been thousands of books published on traits such as these.

But to win *with* others, not only do we have to demonstrate a healthy balance of the above traits but we also need to develop an understanding of the additional principles that mark the profile of an authentic Double Winner.

The following traits are among the most important that differentiate the win-win individual from the rest of society. I have not ranked them in any special order of importance. That is for you to do, according to your own unique perspective.

Double Winners Enjoy the Game

Robert Morelli, a colleague of mine who often shares his own win-win philosophy with me, sent me his helpful book *Winning*, in which he refers to the well-known poem that concludes with the thought, "It's not whether you win or lose, it's how you play the game."

Morelli observes that few of us really understand the depth of meaning in this simple rhyme. The poet is not simply talking about being a good sport. His real message is that the person who plays any game with the intention of enjoying the game itself, regardless of the outcome, *always wins.*

All of us yearn to seek our destinies and spend our lives in our own ways. Double Winners do not let their first paying job out of high school or college determine their profession for the rest of their lives. They listen to the counsel of their elders and consider the opinions of their peers, but they don't let their parents, their professors, and their friends decide which career path they should take.

Double Winners don't let economics alone influence their long-range decisions. They have learned that much of the frustration, depression, and restlessness in society is related to talents that are not being used or properly expressed. Double Winners explore their potential, learn what they are "good at," and make life a "hobby" that they pursue with gusto and eagerness as if every day were Saturday.

Double Winners pass up the "TGIF" ritual of looking forward to the end of another dull week. I was reminded of this when I visited the Sony Corporation's color TV set assembly facility in Southern California not long ago and noticed a sign on the bulletin board: "Thank God It's Monday, Another Week to Enjoy and Excel."

Double Winners enjoy living seven-sevenths of the week. They look forward to relaxing and renewing on the weekend. But, like the Japanese have taught them, Double Winners say, "TGIM. Thank God It's Monday."

Double Winners Have Purpose Beyond Self

One of the most fundamental and important aspects of the Double Win is an understanding of the necessity for human purpose. The human system is teleological, or goal-seeking, by design. Given random thoughts or fixed on an unrealistic idea too far out of sight, the human system will wander aimlessly around its world until it wears itself out or self-destructs, just like an unguided missile.

People who are not practicing the Double Win let life happen to them—going to their place of business to see what happens, just "showing up," getting through the day. Their minds store vague images of a peaceful world, inflation and deficit-free, with eventual retirement to a Greek island and a fortune hidden in Switzerland. They wait for the ship of fate that will deliver them to that rich port. They try their luck in Vegas and Atlantic City, or wait for the mailman to bring them their windfall from publishers' sweepstakes.

However, the Double Winner thinks twice about life—and retirement—without goals or purpose. Insurance industry actuaries have found that retired businessmen and women, military personnel, and pensioners—on fixed incomes, with no challenges, in full retirement, after thirty years in the work force—last an average of seven years. Not much time to enjoy the good life and do nothing.

In my own studies of prisoners of war, I was shocked at the relationship between lack of purpose and disease, emotional and physical atrophy, "turncoating," and death. I was equally amazed at the apparent direct relationship between specificity of purpose and "reasons" for living with emotional and physical well-being, and survival. What struck me the most was that the goal-oriented or "purposeful" prisoners of war were identified by their captors and quickly isolated. Although they were beaten, starved, and degraded like the lowest of animals, they lived through the horror *better* than the prisoners put in the minimum-security camps, who had food, shelter, diversions, and who went through the duration of the war just "being there."

We all have an opportunity and potential for success in our lives, and it takes just as much effort and energy to lead a bad life as it does to lead a good life. And yet, millions lead unhappy, aimless lives, existing from day to day, year to year, confused and frustrated in a prison of their own making. They are POWs, too! Prisoners of work, prisoners of wishes, and prisoners of their world.

Losers are the people who have never made the decisions that could set them free. They have not decided what to do with their lives. They go out each day to see what happens. And because they are not really committed, they rush to escape each evening and on the weekends from a "have to" world, instead of participating fully in a "plan to" world.

Since the mind is a very specific biocomputer, it needs specific instructions and directions. The reason most people never reach their goals is that they don't define them, learn about them, or even seriously consider them as believable or achievable. Double Winners can tell you where they're going, what they plan to do along the way, who'll be sharing the adventure with them, and how their plans will benefit others. God is the great Architect and each of us are builders. We need to build our lives by discovering our natural abilities, learning new skills, emulating healthy role models, and following a plan of action that will stand the test of time and external forces.

Double Winners live on purpose, and then go one step further. Part of their secret for vital, vibrant feelings about their goals is that they are reaching out beyond themselves for meaning. I was watching the "Today" show one morning, and my attention was captured by an interview between Jane Pauley and a "Mr. Smith" who was celebrating his 102nd birthday. Mr. Smith had brought his potted plants and was proudly referring to them as his "upstarts" during the brief conversation.

Jane Pauley was becoming a bit frustrated. Time was running out and all Mr. Smith was doing was making a fuss over his chrysanthemums and night-blooming cirrus. Jane tried to bring him back to the main point. "But Mr. Smith, we all would really like to know to what you attribute your long life." Mr. Smith, not the least bit senile, still went ahead showing off and talking about his flowers. He touched them, watered them, and concentrated on them while the audience watched and listened patiently at one hundred thousand dollars per minute.

"This little lovely won't bloom for another two years," he chuckled, as Jane made one last attempt, before the cutaway to a commercial, to discover his elixir for longevity.

"What's your secret for living so long and staying so active?" The old man replied with a question of his own: "Who would take care of these beautiful flowers?"

Jane sighed, turned a little pink, and "Today" took a time-out to sell something. I could only hope that some viewers had gotten Mr. Smith's point. He might grow flowers that his own eyes would never see in full bloom, but he had just given millions the secret of longevity—for free. *Have a purpose that will outlive you!* Create something beautiful for others. And give it away for free.

Double Winners Earn the Respect of Others

Along with enjoying the game and having a transcending purpose, Double Winners also extend a strong hand to other human beings who are reaching, groping, or just trying to hang on.

One of my favorite mentors and friends was the late Hans Selye, acknowledged "stress" pioneer. He condensed his philosophy of life into four simple words: "Earn thy neighbor's love."

By making a constant effort to win the respect and gratitude of others, our homes will be storehouses full of happiness. The more we modify our win-lose selfishness, the more acceptance we gain from others. The more acceptance we have, the safer we feel, and the less negative stress we need to experience.

Rather than trying to accumulate money and power, Double Winners acquire goodwill by doing things that help their neighbors win.

Several years ago, the Greater New York Council of the Boy Scouts of America started with two thousand handicapped children and sought to determine whether these kids could "make it as Boy Scouts."

The New York Times took a look at Troop 887 and its leader, Max Fuchs, in class at P.S. 19 on New York's Lower East Side. The youngsters had IQs under 50. Most were totally nonverbal; a few could "sign" to communicate. As they came to class, Mr. Fuchs and an assistant put a cap on each one and helped him into a tee shirt with Boy Scout insignias. With grunts and waving arms, they vied for the time-honored privilege of holding the flags. As the National Anthem, Pledge of Allegiance, the Scout Oath, and the Scout Laws led off the meeting, the kids tried to stay with it, even if they could only say a word or two. Mr. Fuchs arranged each boy's right hand in the Scout salute.

Then the room was darkened, and a mounted electric light on the floor was the "campfire." Hot dogs and beans were warmed on a hot plate, simulating the thrice-per-year cookouts at a real Scout camp on Staten Island. After "chow," Mr. Fuchs showed the boys how to make floating compasses with corks and magnetized needles. They moved around the room, watching or feeling the needles change direction.

The short-term goal of the exercise was to teach manual dexterity, motor skills, and a sense of achievement. For almost any effort, these special Scouts were recognized with a treasured badge or bead. The long-term goal was, of course, to try and "mainstream" the kids; to help them learn to be with nonhandicapped peers.

How did the original experiment work out? Today, there are seventy-five thousand Boy Scouts within New York City and nearly one-third of them are disabled: blind, deaf, autistic, mentally retarded, or, in many instances, enduring a combination of these difficulties. Nearly all are now participants in Scouting for the Handicapped, mostly in special-education classes in the 350 public schools where Scouting is part of their regular schoolwork.[1]

Naturally, no program is necessarily perfect. Parents of normal kids might argue that their children aren't getting sufficient attention due to all the time spent on needs of the "special" Scouts. Some Scout leaders may not want the extra work involved. Why bother? Why not teach normal kids and forget about roasting hot dogs over hot plates in darkened classrooms? Is it worth it, being a "show and tell" example to kids who have to limp and grope their way into the mainstream of life?

Double Winners know the answer. It is not possessing eyes that see, ears that hear, or a body that functions properly that creates the win. Success is in the act of offering insight, outreach, and function to others who might otherwise never know the thrill of accomplishment. Satisfaction is in helping others become winners, instead of just vegetating. The payoff is in the giving.

Double Winners Practice Synergism

Entrophy occurs when things wear out from use. Atrophy is when things wither from lack of use. Synergism happens when things work better as they are used. The principle behind synergism, simply stated, is: "The whole is greater than the sum of its parts."

Anthropologist Ruth Benedict, working in the 1930s and 1940s, classified entire societies of people as high or low in synergism. Her high-synergism societies were those where people cooperated and worked together for mutual advantage. Benedict's low-synergism societies were populated by individuals with the win-lose philosophy, where virtue suffered and class distinction flourished.

My own observation of synergism in action became keenly focused when I became involved with the United States Olympic Movement in 1980. As a member of the USOC Sports Medicine

Council, my interest has been in the psychology of coaching and developing mental attitudes to enhance high performance.

One of the best case studies was our ice hockey team, which was training to compete in the Winter Games at Lake Placid, New York. Coach Herb Brooks wanted adaptable individuals who could work together better than their opponents. He used a special psychological test to select his final team. Rather than trying to assemble superstars, he sought team players who could respond effectively to pressure.

The U.S. team was ranked seventh in the eight-team field for the 1980 Winter Games, and had the toughest schedule. To add to the impossibility of the situation, they had been trounced, 10 to 3, by the Soviets at Madison Square Garden in their final exhibition game.

With the deck stacked against them, the Americans were willing to dare to try. With each game, they appeared to gain new energy and confidence. First came Sweden, and down they went to defeat. Next it was Norway, then the Czechs, followed by Rumania, and finally West Germany. The outcomes were the same. The U.S. team drew from some hidden reservoir of stamina and won, always with a scoring burst in the third period.

And then came the crucial match. All that really stood between the Americans and a gold medal was the Russian team that had made mincemeat of them only days before. Many hockey observers were quite sure the Russian skaters could compete quite handily in the NHL. For the American kids to be taking them on was something tantamount to a semipro football team squaring off with the Los Angeles Raiders. But the impossible happened. When the third-period horn sounded, it was U.S. 4 and U.S.S.R. 3!

Forget about the odds and the exhibition defeats—this was their moment in history. There were twenty of them, averaging twenty-two years of age. As individuals, they were good. As a team, they were a synergistic winning machine that became the best ice hockey team in the world in 1980.

Athletics is only one field in which synergism can be a productive force. Over the centuries, the Japanese have developed a "circular management" approach, which guides a company in decision making by seeking consensus throughout the organization. This concept demands that many more people participate in key decisions, meaning more parts contribute to the work of the whole.

Circular management works well in Japan, a culture that teaches the humility and submission needed to get consensus in a group. It does not fare as well in America and other Western nations which encourage the independence and challenge to authority that make gaining a consensus difficult.

We are, however, seeing more and more Double Win synergism occurring in other areas of American business. The big three auto makers are adding labor representatives to their boards of directors. Several major corporations, especially airlines, are sharing ownership in stock and other representation in lieu of salary incentives. One newer airline, America West, used a campaign advertising the claim that it served its customers better because it was employee-owned. Eastern Airlines commercials have made the same proud boast.

The key to synergism in any group is that if you own a piece of the action, if you feel as if you are a part of a winning machine and that you really count, you do everything you can to increase productivity. Synergism is a key ingredient in any Double Win.

Double Win Communication: "I'll Make Them Glad"

You cannot be a Double Winner without win-win communication. Win-lose communicators seldom really listen. Double Winners are masters of the art of listening, which is the most positive demonstration of expressing value to another. They know that listeners learn a great deal, while talkers learn nothing. Double Winners ask questions. They draw the other person out. They ask for examples. They feed back what others have just said for clarity and understanding.

Not long ago, I gave a seminar to Murata Erie North America, Inc., an unusually successful industrial company consisting, for the most part, of American and European managers and employees, but owned by a Japanese conglomerate. At dinner with Murata's president, Fred Chanoki, I asked him what he thought was one of the major assets of the Japanese in successfully managing large numbers of employees. As part of his answer, Mr. Chanoki shared with me from a speech given in April of 1984 by Makoto Kikuchi, Director of the Sony Corporation Research Center, to the Japanese press. Here are excerpts from his remarks:

"Japan's educational system fosters the capacity to digest vast quantities of knowledge in a very short time. This accounts for our rapid advances in technology. Even more important in our success, perhaps, is the ability of the Japanese to suppress their individual egos, making them open to receive others' ideas and know-how. This principle is basic to the teaching of Japan's traditional arts, where the disciple must absorb the method of his master."[2]

In other words, a big part of communication is developing the discipline to listen to others, to pay them value, by being receptive to what they have to say.

Some master communicators believe that "paying value to another" is the greatest communication skill of all. One of my own mentors was Earl Nightingale, who taught me the advantages of communicating with an "I'll make them glad they talked to me" attitude. This great idea is so simple that it's almost deceptive. We have to examine it carefully to understand how it works and why.

"I'll make them glad" is an attitude that can become a whole way of life. When Double Winners deal with a prospect, an adversary, or a potential friend, their attitude is service-oriented, not self-oriented. Their concern is for the other person, not themselves. When we have other people's interests at heart, not just our own, the others can sense it. They may not be able to put into words why they feel that way, but they do.

On the other hand, people get an uneasy feeling when they talk with individuals who have only their own interest in mind and not theirs. There's an excellent reason we all get these feelings about people. It's known as nonverbal communication. It's the old business of speaking so loudly that no one can hear what you're saying! And it's tremendously important to all of us in practicing the Double Win.

Roger Rowe, Master Communicator

One of the most impressive Double Winners in communication I've ever encountered is the principal of our youngest daughter's school. Lisa is an eighth-grader at the Rancho Santa Fe School in California, where about 440 students from kindergarten through eighth grade are lovingly guided toward high school by Dr. Roger

Rowe. It's the only school I know where neither kids nor parents look forward to graduation.

Roger Rowe's approach is legendary in our county, maybe even in our country. His stated philosophy of education is:

> "To be aware of the uniqueness of each individual and to treat that uniqueness with loving concern. To provide each student with the opportunities appropriate to his or her abilities and interests. To encourage each one to develop an 'I will, I can' attitude. To help kids go a step above and beyond what they themselves, or even others, might normally expect of them. And, not be surprised when they do."[3]

Dr. Rowe practices what he preaches. As a father of two daughters who have gone the distance under his guidance, I almost wish I was back in grammar school. Roger Rowe actually knows, by name, every student he has ever supervised or taught for over twenty-six years! He communicates on a first-name basis with every student and every parent. He knows how individual fifth-graders scored on their math tests today and how all the second-graders did in their poem project yesterday. He calls monthly to congratulate us on Lisa's honor-roll performance. In the same conversation, he asks how our other daugher, Kim, is doing as a junior in high school.

His office is open to students and parents alike. And they use it. By his total concern for the other person, by his genuine effort to know each individual and his or her special needs, he has fostered an incredible spirit of cooperation between himself, his staff, his students, and their parents. The results speak for themselves. The school is a smoothly running operation and the students and teachers are a well-balanced, motivated, happy group of individuals. Behavior problems and the incidence of drug abuse is extremely low. Good scholarship and citizenship abound. And, before they graduate from the eighth grade, most of the kids are able to pass the same test required of high-school seniors to earn their diplomas!

Roger Rowe is a master of the "I'll make them glad they talked with me" attitude, the idea of helping other people solve their problems by having their interests at heart. Everybody wins with this attitude. And that's Double Win communication.

Double Winners Don't Trumpet Status

Double Winners don't need to show off. In our status-hungry society, a certain kind of house, car, clothing, or other possessions are symbols the win-lose individual uses in a superficial attempt to tell the rest of the world how important he is. Even more important than telling others who they are, these exterior standards of living serve to remind them who they are. Like Narcissus, they are as beautiful.

There is a strong relationship between win-lose living and materialism. This is evidenced by a growing tendency to display an array of expensive possessions and outward trappings of affluence. With the easy credit of the eighties and the flood of plastic charge cards, almost anyone with a steady job can display a foreign sports car, a power boat, or a camper in the driveway.

Win-lose advocates often glorify and encourage the display of worldly goodies because they think it conveys a successful image. Actually, the concentration on status symbols is more likely to say to others that the owner may be lacking in self-esteem. The person with strong self-respect can afford to project a modest image. Although all of us have the right to enjoy the very best quality in everything we purchase, I believe it shows a much better sense of value to buy things that endure and are pleasing to me, not things that are simply expensive so I can impress others with their price tags. The Double Winner is the one who projects success by the unassuming way he or she lives, plays, and works with others.

For instance, Double Winners don't brag. People who trumpet their exploits and shout for service are actually calling for help. The showboats, braggarts, and blowhards are desperate for attention to make up for inadequate internal values. I have observed juvenile delinquents try to be cool, swaggering, and macho. Methinks they protest too loudly, however, because beneath the tough exterior shell is a soft individual who secretly wants to be noticed and important. It is said that the infamous criminal John Dillinger ran into a farmhouse and repeatedly yelled at the occupants, "My name is John Dillinger. I'm not going to hurt you; I just wanted you to know that my name is John Dillinger."

And the nonplussed farmer's wife replied, "Now that we know

your name, wipe your feet, state your business, and be on your way. We've got butter to churn!"

Double Winners can project their value without shouting it. They may not always be able to afford to buy the most expensive things, but they always do the very best with the things they can afford. What I've always said is that I may not be the best looking in the group, but in my own way, I'll always be trying to look my best in the group.

The toys and trappings of affluence and material success tell nothing really important about who we are and how we live. Double Winners let their actions, not their possessions, do the talking. If you've got the real thing, you won't have to flaunt an expensive imitation.

Double Winners "Never Lose"

One of the greatest traits of Double Winners is that they actually win while losing. They know that you can learn more from your failures and mistakes than you can from your victories. One of the most encouraging and heartening things I've found in my studies of people and of life—the Vietnam prisoners-of-war, the Iranian hostages, people going through personal tragedies—is that failures can be jumping-off points to future successes. I'm constantly reminded of the old but wisdom-laden quote: "The only difference between stumbling blocks and stepping-stones is the way we use them."

In *The Sky's the Limit*, Wayne Dyer discusses the difference between the external and internal approach to winning. If you must always defeat some kind of opponent to be a winner, you are using an external scale. Dyer prefers to shoot for the goal of being a "No Limit" person, for whom winning is always an internal process.[4]

Dyer believes that the only way to stop thinking of yourself as a loser is to go beyond the win-lose dichotomy. He also believes you can begin developing a winning attitude about everything without kidding yourself. The first step is to discard the well-known win-lose attitude that neatly labels people winners or losers because of how they come out in specific competition. "The total winning attitude," writes Dyer, "is one which allows you to think of yourself as a winner all the time, while still giving yourself room to grow."[5]

With the winning attitude, you don't have to kick yourself because an opponent is more skillful (or perhaps luckier) than you are on a given day. You don't have to judge yourself for failing to meet a goal you may have set. You don't have to look at others to see how you match up as a human being. Indeed, you never ". . . have to use comparison in order to measure your own self-worth."[6]

I see Dyer's "inner winner" as the inward character of the Double Winner. It is not a question of avoiding all competition. That is impossible. And, as Dyer points out, always defeating others in competition is equally impossible. You simply can't win them all, but what you can do is learn from every experience and make it motivation for growth, rather than more proof that you just don't have it. What we need to do is get ourselves ". . . out of the self-defeating pattern that is so prevalent in our culture, the attitude that stresses winning as a result of defeating losers." In other words, junk the win-lose attitude. Go for the Double Win from within!

From Drug Addict to Double Winner

"Nice theory," you might be saying. "How does it work?" How about the highly competitive field of professional sports? Micheal Ray Richardson was traded to the New Jersey Nets basketball team in February 1983. He performed poorly the rest of the season and, during the following summer, he was put on suspension due to a cocaine problem. The Nets reinstated him in December of 1983, but only because of pressure from the NBA and the players' union. Richardson claimed he was cured, but many in the Nets organization, including the coach and several players, opposed his return. One player threatened to ask to be traded.

But Richardson hung in there. The rules? Undergo urinalysis three times a week. If even a *trace* of drugs was found, suspension for life.

It was all rather humbling for a proud athlete, good enough to star in the NBA, but Richardson played by the rules and by the following February he won back his starting position. He led the team in steals, led the guards in rebounds, and averaged only 2.4 turnovers per game while leading the Nets fast break.

An excellent outside shooter, Richardson can also drive the lane and was always a threat to score. With his help, the Nets won nineteen of their last twenty-seven regular season games and stunned the world champion Philadelphia 76ers in the play-offs before bowing to Milwaukee in the second round.

Said a Nets executive: "For me, he has redefined the enormous potential of the human spirit. The light had almost gone out in the tunnel for him. But through sheer perseverance on his part, he has succeeded like few could have. . . . I can honestly give him all the credit. Sure, he had help. But he's been the driving force."

And what is Richardson's perception of all this newfound success? He says his wife gave him strength: "She was always thinking positive." He is also grateful for the support of his teammates, who are now on his side. Most significant, however, is this Double Winner observation: "You have to face the things you cannot change. There are certain things that are stronger than you, things that you have to face. That was one of them. And I faced it."

To face the things that are stronger and not let them label you a loser. To face failure in a highly competitive athletic jungle like NBA basketball and use it as motivation to grow. These are the traits of the inner winner Wayne Dyer describes. Yes, Micheal Ray Richardson had plenty of external standards being laid upon him by team statisticians who kept track of everything from shots made to how many times he sneezed. But he operated on internal standards that said, "You blew it with drugs, but you are no loser. You can turn it around."

And turn it around he did. Richardson scored wins when he got reinstated and fought his way back to starter and star contributor to a winning team. But look at the "wins" he gave back:

> His teammates had a floor leader who helped take them to the play-offs.
>
> His employers have proof that it pays (in more than "good press") to give an employee another chance.
>
> His wife has been rewarded for her support of a husband who was anything but a "good risk."
>
> People everywhere have encouragement that you can whip the curse of cocaine addiction.[7]

Micheal Ray Richardson is a Double Winner, for whom failure was an important—but temporary—learning experience.

How Abe and Edison Scored Double Wins

History is full of examples of those who built upon losses to achieve great victories. Certainly one of the most dramatic examples in the field of politics is that of Abraham Lincoln, who endured an unparalleled record of defeats but was seasoned by them to become the one man of heart and vision able to preserve the union and bind up its wounds. Abe's string of losses began in 1832 with the loss of his job as a shopkeeper, followed by a defeat in a state legislative race. In 1833, he was appointed postmaster but had to supplement his income with other jobs. A successful bid for the legislature in '34 was followed by losses in '38, running for Speaker, and in '43, running for U.S. Congress. His eventual election to Congress in '46 was followed by a defeat and removal in '48. From 1849 to 1858, the list went on: defeats for land officer, the Senate, the vice presidential nomination, and the Senate again! But Lincoln learned from every defeat—and changed the course of American history with his election as president of the United States in 1860.

Thomas Edison is well-known for his inventions such as the electric light bulb and the phonograph. Less well known, perhaps, is his tenacity in the face of what looked like failure. He tried five thousand different materials while seeking a filament that would make the electric light work. Did he see that as five thousand failures? No—instead, he called it "succeeding in learning five thousand different things that would not work!"

But the light bulb was nothing, compared to his efforts to invent a storage battery. After *twenty-five thousand* attempts with no results, someone asked him how it felt to fail so badly. He replied again: "Failure? I'm not a failure at all. I now know twenty-five thousand ways *not* to make a battery."

The Double Winner never labels lack of success as "failure." He or she takes advantage of lessons learned while losing, and keeps moving toward the goal. Truly, in the long run, Double Winners never lose.

Double Winners Use the Spiritual Dimension

Perhaps more important than any other part of the Double Winner's profile is the tremendous ability to tap the abundance beyond ourselves—the spiritual dimension.

Double Winners see their total person in such a fully formed perspective that it gives them a good idea of how they fit into the "big picture" of life. They have learned to know themselves intimately, even as they are known. They have learned to feel one with their Creator and with the universe. They have learned to be aware of time and their opportunity to learn from the past. They plan the future, while living as fully as possible in the present.

One of the most fascinating examples of the power of the spiritual dimension that I have found comes from Dr. Herbert Benson, Head Cardiologist at Boston's Beth Israel Hospital, a main teaching facility of the Harvard Medical School. Benson is the author of the best-selling book *The Relaxation Response,* which extols and teaches the benefits of meditation.

In an interview with Daniel Goleman, Benson admitted that his book got people interested in meditating, but that many couldn't stick with it. After an initial burst of enthusiasm, they just couldn't find time to spend ten to twenty minutes a day repeating some neutral sound or word in meditation. Benson started asking his readers and patients if they would rather use a prayer. Many said they would and when they tried it, they found they were more likely to stick with the meditative relaxation process.

One example was a retired shopkeeper who consulted one of Benson's colleagues for a very rapid heartbeat. The doctor suggested meditating while repeating the number one as his focusing sound. The man soon returned, his condition worse than ever. For some reason, the number one had a very negative effect. In the course of the conversation, the shopkeeper commented that he was of the Greek Orthodox faith. The doctor suggested that he use the Greek words *Kyrie eleison* ("Lord, have mercy") while meditating. The man, who believed deeply in the prayer, started meditating with it twice a day and soon had his heart rate under control.[8]

Dr. Benson commented that people in Western cultures have difficulty with repeating neutral words or sounds (what Hinduism and other Eastern religions call "mantras"), but they do much better with prayer phrases from their own faith. The point may also be that prayer, as opposed to meditation, has an object beyond the inward self: God. Prayer is by nature a method of connection and communication, a fundamental aspect of the Double Win.

For example, Roman Catholics might use "Lord Jesus Christ, have mercy," or a line from the Lord's Prayer. Protestants might use teachings by Jesus, such as "My peace I give unto you" (John 14:27), or a teaching from the Apostle Paul, "The peace of God, which passeth all understanding . . ." (Philippians 4:7). Jews and Christians alike could use the Hebrew word for peace ("shalom") or phrases from the Psalms, such as "Thy word is a lamp unto my feet . . ." (Psalms 119:105).

In the same interview, which appeared in *American Health* magazine, Dr. Benson observed:

> Illness can be treated more successfully if a patient really believes (trusts) in a particular cure.
> A drug given by an enthusiastic doctor is far more potent than one given by a skeptical doctor.
> A patient may be able to get better without a doctor by calling on his belief in the spiritual dimension.
> In 25 percent of ailments, drugs and surgery are effective, but in the other 75 percent, a person's beliefs can play a powerful role. "Medicine and faith," says Benson, "can work hand in hand."

As Daniel Goleman concluded his interview with Dr. Benson, he commented, "In a way, this brings religion back into medicine."

Benson replied: "Frequently, my patients say, 'Thank you, doctor, for telling me to pray again. I wanted to, but felt funny about it.' "[9]

These insights from a recognized medical doctor may seem startling to some and rather old hat to others. Many people have relied on prayer and faith all their lives, no matter what their doctors might think about it.

Double Winners invest in unswerving faith beyond self, and beyond relationships with other human beings. They not only understand their connection to those who went before them in the past and to those who will inherit their world in the future; they also are intimately involved with the One who shapes the entire universe.

As I speak to groups in every kind of setting, I talk to people who have different ideas on what or who this divine order is. My own point of reference is the Bible. As a Christian, the cornerstone of my life is my faith in the divine Creator, in whom I live and move and have my being. My relationship to God spurs me toward the reality of dreams that I hope for but can't actually see or touch. To make my dreams reality, I don't waste time despairing, I get busy caring. Instead of accumulating power, I try to distribute optimism.

Somebody has said, "Don't curse the darkness, light a candle."[10] I believe that, and I also believe that the only way you can light a candle in the darkness around you is to have your own candles of faith burning brightly around you in your soul.

Completing the Double Win Profile

Many other characteristics of a Double Winner could be described in an attempt to draw a complete profile. You may have thought of other qualities that are particuarly important to you. But perhaps no one could ever draw the complete picture. The important thing to grasp in profiling the Double Winner is to understand you are nothing more than the total picture you have of yourself through your own thoughts and actions. In other words, the composite element in the profile of the Double Winner is his or her self-image. Self-esteem is the basic foundation for developing a Double Win attitude toward life.

Self-esteem is that deep-down, inside-the-skin feeling of your own worth: "You know, I like myself. I really do like myself. Given my parents and my background, I'm glad I'm me. I'd rather be me than anyone else, living or at any time in history." This is the self-talk of a winner, and positive self-talk is the key to developing self-esteem. Winners develop strong beliefs of self-worth and self-confidence through learning to tolerate or handle the thorns, in order to savor the fragrance of the rose.

So important is self-esteem that we'll devote the next three chapters to giving it a closer look. As we will see, the would-be Double Winner has a formidable opponent to conquer: a society and culture that is basically tuned to the win-lose life. After years of traveling and talking in the interest of helping people succeed in life, I am firmly convinced that our predominantly win-lose treatment of each other is a major reason for the epidemic of low self-esteem found today in all strata of society.

But I believe we can turn it all around. Life is not really a rat race to come in first. That's win-lose thinking at its "finest." The Double Win life is stopping along the way to live every moment to the hilt, always looking for ways to share your wins with others. The Double Winner has enough self-esteem to know he or she can come in last and still be first. The rest of this book discusses why and how all this can work in anyone's life.

LOSERS	WINNERS	DOUBLE WINNERS
Seek attention	Seek admiration	Earn respect

PART II

Your Self-Esteem: Bedrock of the Double Win

The Double Win appears simple on the surface. Read a self-help book or two. Learn about the qualities of a win-win person and then go out and succeed. After all, what's so hard about applying "If I let the other person win, I win, too"?

Actually, quite a bit.

Before we can successfully practice "simple" Double Win precepts, we have to recognize three major hurdles that stand in our way:

1. The win-lose philosophy is natural.
2. The win-lose philosophy is dominant in our society.
3. The win-lose philosophy is habit-forming and addicting.

We all live in a culture that is basically dedicated to the win-lose philosophy. It's a point of view that is natural enough. No one blames you for "looking out for Number One" as long as you are discreet and law-abiding about it.

The Double Win, however, is unnatural. The Double Win attitude requires self-examination, understanding, self-discipline, and maturity.

Above all, it takes high self-esteem. The next three chapters talk about why you need a good self-image—and how to get it.

4

The Win-Lose Child of Your Past

As infants, we are preoccupied with meeting our own needs. We want self-gratification—immediately. Most early communications are used to manipulate others into pleasuring us. With increasing frustration, we grudgingly recognize the existence of the needs of others. But throughout childhood, we view the needs of others as tools, trade-offs, and other "quid pro quos" to get what we want.

The Adolescent Adult

As we enter adolescence, we ingeniously attempt to maintain the self-centered privileges of a dependent child while demanding the right to do our thing on our own terms. The old cliché fits the adolescent mentality perfectly: "I have my cake and I'm eating it, too, a la mode!"

Once we enter adulthood, however, we put all that foolishness behind us, right? Wrong. Many adults live their entire lives at an emotional level that ranges from childlike to adolescent. The chief symptom? Preoccupation with the immediate gratification of self and its senses. The child's rationale is an uninhibited "If it feels good, do it!" The adolescent approach climbs a bit higher on the ladder to say: "If it feels good, do it, as long as you don't hurt anybody else." This adolescent rationale is held by many adults who go their win-lose way "doing what comes naturally."

The "Natural" Isn't Always Healthy

The admission that win-lose living is natural doesn't mean that it is healthy, or that it will help society thrive and endure in the long run. Earthquakes, floods, anger, violence, and the "fight or flight" response are also natural though not necessarily healthy phenomena. M. Scott Peck observes that we have to teach ourselves to do the unnatural through self-discipline. He believes that the thing which makes us most human is "our capacity to do the unnatural, to transcend and hence transform our own nature."[1]

I agree with Peck and would only add that one of the joys of being human is our God-given ability to learn to relate to our environment more creatively, rather than continue to blunder and plunder along, following primitive instincts. Of course, there is no way to quantitatively keep score, to tell precisely when we are doing win-lose or win-win living. Human behavior cannot be so easily classified or formularized. There are ways, however, to measure quality of life, to tell when we are moving toward the win-lose (hedonistic and narcissistic) or the win-win (caring and sharing with no eye to a payoff).

Some tip-offs that reveal the win-lose approach include:

- caring for others only to the extent that those others provide you with self-gratification ("What can she do for *me?*")
- enjoying relationships only so long as they do not compromise selfish needs ("I'll love you *if* or *when. . . .*")
- withdrawing into materialism, the possession of things, which creates the fantasy of success in a vain hope to banish frustration and emptiness ("Yes, I paid a bundle for it, but it's only money.")
- wanting to pay as little as possible for pleasure and fulfillment ("There must be a free ride in this somewhere.")

The win-win life-style is the antithesis of the above. The win-win person is prepared to pay the price of some self-deprivation in the cause of caring for others. No one is capable of giving love unconditionally all the time, because the natural win-lose (look out for Number One) attitude is always in the way. But an encouraging sign of true maturity and love is that you're increasingly willing to devote more time and effort to caring for others than trying to satisfy your own real or imagined needs. This is the Double Win, and it doesn't come naturally!

The Bombardment of Win-Lose Role Models

With all of its "natural" qualities, it is no wonder the win-lose philosophy is being taught throughout society as the way to the top. Win-lose role models dominate every medium of human expression, particularly television and films. Television, one of the greatest technological gifts ever given to mankind, is, for the most part, in the hands of commercial powers who are primarily interested in making money. Win-lose programming, filled with violence, escapism, and banality, is holding sway, and one can only hope for better days ahead. The potential Double Win learning opportunities afforded by television are unparalleled in history.

The good news is that, in most areas, television service has been expanded to thirty-six or more broadcast channels. The major networks will be increasingly challenged by more innovative programming, promoting intellectual, cultural, and spiritual growth. I am hoping there will be a balancing shift from mostly "entertainment" to more of what I call "educainment," as we begin really caring about and sharing with others in a process of mutual enrichment.

Meanwhile, the bad news reigns almost supreme. All day long, we are bombarded with programs that report murder, mayhem, and disaster. Why such stress on the morbid and negative? Why not give a little more time to balance the wrong with the right?

Perhaps the answer lies in a cynical old cliché about the fire burning another's home warming those who aren't the victims.

Television news programmers are paid well to know what sells. They know fully well that the need to be shocked or titillated is greater than the need to be informed or inspired. The same psychology is what makes a crowd gather at a fight or an accident. But have you ever seen a crowd assemble to watch a Boy Scout help an old lady cross the street?

Beauty and the "Best"

But the problem only begins with the newscasts. A glut of so-called dramas, sit-coms, and movies provides us with role models who are either superheroes with unnatural strength, superhuman abilities, and exaggerated and expanded reflexes, or they are incompetent, uncouth, bumbling, or criminally insane. Glance through the TV listings and watch so many leading players fall neatly into these categories. Casual observation of television role models also reveals that, usually, the good guys are white professionals. Working-class individuals, foreigners, and minorities are usually absent or play comic or negatively stereotyped roles.

Naturally, beauty is largely based on external characteristics. The ideal woman has the face of Christie Brinkley, the figure of Victoria Principal, and the charming feistiness of Jane Fonda. Her male counterpart looks like Tom Selleck or O. J. Simpson, and has the moves of John Travolta or Michael Jackson.

The inevitable result is an American public preoccupied with appearances and immediate sensual gratification, which identifies winning with looking young and beautiful, or having fame and fortune. It is not surprising that so many people become either apathetic or cynical about self-improvement and personal development. Because they are guided by external standards set by others, they often raise their sights unrealistically high to begin with. They want the American dream they saw on TV and they want it now. They say, "Give me something I can swallow, quick!"

Perhaps the worst subliminal impression given by TV-style reality is that people are also commodities—only the new model is acceptable.

And Don't Forget That Word From the Sponsor

As if the main events weren't enough—with soaps to wash our brains and "smut-coms" to "spice" our lives—TV commercials play a strong role in our expectations, attitudes, value systems, eating habits, and relationships with friends and family. Be aware that those little minidramas, immortalizing great literary genius like "Ring around the collar!" and "Tastes great—less filling," sell to the tune of one hundred thousand dollars to three hundred thousand dollars per minute. Why are they so expensive? Because they come to you when you are most receptive and ready to be sold.

As you relax, the rhythmic repetitions flow in and the message is powerful. That message says material goods and leisure activities are the only significant sources of happiness. In direct contrast to the idea that a strong self-image is independent of external possessions, we are led to believe that all of life's problems can be solved by products or services in about sixty seconds.

To live the Double Win in a win-lose environment, we need to realize that TV programming is dictated by win-lose individuals who are more interested in immediate-profit gratification than in the side effects of their products. The television and motion picture industries produce their own brand of toxic waste, every bit as damaging as the chemical kind. DDT is matched by MTV. X rays give cancer, X-rated films produce malignancies in minds. There is polluted H_2O and polluted HBO. And we seem to forget that the mind can be damaged by expediency as easily as the body—perhaps more so.

As We Thinketh, So We Are

Admittedly, all of this sounds pretty grim. My wife found this chapter on the desk, and after reading it, she frantically started switching channels, trying to find the local educational offering.

"Okay, okay, Waitley, I'll be good," she muttered. "But can I keep 'Dynasty' just to admire Crystal's wardrobe?"

"Oh, all right, you can have 'Dynasty,' " I replied. "I can understand. As an old three-sport jock, it's hard for me not to catch 'Monday Night Football' now and then. It will be nice, however, to have you join me more often for 'Masterpiece Theater' and 'Charles Kuralt'."

Lisa, our youngest, was listening and started getting nervous about all this talk of giving up TV shows. "Please—don't censor 'Happy Days,' 'Different Strokes,' and 'Webster.' I promise to do my homework, feed the cat, take out the trash—"

"Enough!" I snorted. "We all should reform. Everybody is sentenced to 'Jacques Cousteau,' 'Wild Kingdom,' and reruns of 'Little House on the Prairie' for a month. And that's final!"

I share that little not-quite-imaginary scene with you to make a

point. Television is part of our lives and we all have *our* favorite
shows, most of which we think are fine. It's the *other* people who are
getting corrupted. *We* have better taste than that!

In every home, we could all argue over what's acceptable and
what's trash. I am not for tossing out all TV sets or dynamiting the
three major networks. They aren't forcing us to watch their offer-
ings, but we do. All of us need constant reminding of how TV is
selling us the win-lose way of life. Television (and cinema) have
become our most powerful sources of role models, providing example after example of criminal violence, moral bankruptcy, and
families falling all over each other in the most pathetic and ridiculous confrontations. Almost all of this is enacted in a win-lose atmosphere, from the game shows to the big games, from Alexis
confronting Blake Carrington to Jack-in-the-Box finding "no comparison" over at McDonald's.

The point I'm trying to make can be summed up in a proverb
from the *Old Testament:* "As a man thinketh in his heart, so is he."[2]
If you look back at my attack on the TV monolith, you'll keep
coming across the term *self-image,* which is really what this chapter
is supposed to cover. Television and movies influence our patterns
of eating, sleeping, dressing, and recreation. They help form our
values, social behavior, and perceptions of the real world. Unfortunately, too many of us exist on a mental diet of TV and motion picture "junk food." Not only is it addictive but it also seems to
produce an insatiable hunger for more, which leads to emotional
malnutrition—and a weakened self-image. In the words of one consumer advocate who has his own show on a West Coast network:
"We've gotta fight back!"

The Inner Winner (or Loser)

There are as many theories about television and learning as there
are learners, but one thought is clear: We learn by observation,
imitation, and repetition. We seize upon role models, observe their
actions, imitate, then become what we see, hear, read, feel, and
touch. No single realization is as important as this in understanding—and dealing with—that little person called your "inner child
of the past." No matter what your age, there is a child in your past.
You are a child grown older. How your parents raised you and how

you have responded to your teachers, peers, and managers have determined—to a large extent—the adult you see in the mirror. As we have seen, TV also has played a major role in the lives of most adults and is playing an even greater role in the lives of almost all children.

It all goes together to form our inner child, sometimes in rather interesting ways. Robert had many reasons for marrying Pauline, and her cooking was in the top ten. It was, therefore, some time before he gathered the nerve to question a strange habit he had noticed: Each time she cooked a ham, she would first cut off both ends. When he finally asked her why, she answered, unhesitatingly, "That's the way my mother did it."

Not totally satisfied, but unwilling to press her further, Bob waited until the next visit to the home of Pauline's parents. He posed the same question to Pauline's mother, and she replied cheerfully, "Why, that's the way *my* mom always cooked it."

Determined to get to the bottom of the culinary mystery, Bob stopped by after work to visit Pauline's grandmother and casually broached the subject: "Why do you cut the ends off a ham before you bake it? I'm just curious," he smiled.

She looked at him suspiciously and replied curtly, "Because my baking dish is too small!"

Just like Robert's wife, we develop many of our behavior patterns through imitating and identifying with the values and attitudes modeled for us in our families. Our socialization process begins here, too, as we learn to function as social beings with appropriate actions and responses. All of these experiences are the foundation of personality and our concept of ourselves—the self-image.

Individuals exposed to a win-lose environment that fails to nurture a positive self-image can be recognized by how they treat themselves and others. With little respect for themselves, how can they properly respect, work with, live with, and care for others? If they grow up constantly having to compare themselves favorably or unfavorably with others, several negative patterns can develop:

They withdraw and view all relationships as threatening.
They attack and constantly try to prove themselves to the world.

They grow arrogant and calloused, trying to hide their lack of confidence behind a mask of conceit and self-assurance.

Our self-image is the total picture of who we think we are, and the camera starts rolling the minute we achieve that first conscious realization that we are living, functioning beings. The camera (our brain) takes pictures fast and furiously throughout life, and every shot is tucked away in a memory file of limitless capacity.

This subjective sense of who we think ourselves to be governs all our actions and controls our destiny. How we feel about ourselves, how we rate our ability to hang in there, survive, and win, and all that we ever do or aspire to do is based on our time-reinforced self-image.

I've had my own struggles with a poor self-image. Even though my parents told me I was special, my peer group in grammar school and junior high told me different. They offered me such nurturing labels as "Buzzard Beak . . . Beaver Teeth . . . Waitley Come Lately . . . Wartly Weakly . . . Dumbo Ears . . . Measle Face . . . and Turtle Breath!"

During my plebe year at Annapolis, the superlatives were lavished on me by several hundred upper-class midshipmen all day long for 325 straight days:

"Mr. Waitley, you couldn't lead a one-cadet parade."

"You're lower than whale barnacles, and they're on the bottom of the ocean."

"If your eyes were any closer together, we'd call you Cyclops."

"What did your face look like before you went through the windshield?"

"You're so dense you couldn't lead a silent prayer!"

As I began to wear the labels others pinned on me, I began playing my own game of "pin the donkey tail on Waitley." My self-talk and self-descriptions became derisive and klutzy:

In response to a birthday gift: "You shouldn't have gone to all this trouble for *me*."

In response to a compliment on a special favor I did for a neighbor's teenage son, "Don't mention it. It was nothing."

In response to a compliment on my necktie, "Think I got some catsup on it."

In response to a compliment on a great golf shot I made, "Yeah, bet I won't do *that* again!"

After a seesaw career of no-win and win-lose canyons and valleys as a young adult, I finally learned to stop associating myself with external labels, negative self-talk, and humiliating self-presentation. In my early thirties, I began to talk affirmatively about my accomplishments and goals, trying to do so modestly and honestly. I began to say, "Thank you," when other people would bestow any value upon me. I began to accept myself as a changing, growing, and worthwhile human being, imperfect but capable of becoming a Double Winner. And I began to feel good about myself.

During the past fifteen years, since I climbed out of my own marginal level of self-esteem, I have devoted most of my time to listening to others declare their own worth or lack of it. I have tried to help them realize that value is in the "doer not the deed" and that the internalization of value is the key to the Double Win. Unless you have internal values, you have nothing of value to give *to* others. Lacking in internal values, you need to take value *from* others.

Getting Back to Our "Comfort Zones"

As I have tried to illustrate from my own youth, we are not born with a self-image. It grows—as do most of our personality features—over time, based on repeated inputs from our environment. The sum total of our past experiences—our successes and failures, our humiliations and triumphs, and the way we have interacted with those around us and who love us—gives us a subjective sense of the sort of person we are.

But there is an important catch. All of our experiences are pieces of input that are colored by our *perceptions,* and, since our perceptions are not necessarily the same as reality, our sense of who we are may miss the mark by a wide margin. Unfortunately, once an idea or belief becomes a perception, it becomes a "truth" for our self-image.

Each link we add to the growing chain of self-image may either strengthen our lives or shackle them more tightly. Control is in our hands. We cannot outgrow these limits we place on ourselves through faulty self-imaging, but we *can* set new limits. We *can* reset our self-image, like an internal thermostat, from no-win or win-lose to win-win.

Each of us has a number of comfort zones or "settings" that we have developed throughout our lives that dictate the amount of *dis*-comfort we are willing to suffer before making adjustments. Reflect, for a moment, on just how many of your behaviors are set into motion when you move out of these comfort zones. "Too much" can motivate as strongly as "too little." On the level of conscious thought, there are any number of examples: how much time we feel comfortable in spending with those around us; how much effort we feel comfortable in expending on our daily tasks at the office or at home; how much money we feel comfortable in spending on our new clothes.

On a physiological level, there are an infinite number of feedback systems that kick into gear when we leave the comfort zone. Much as a thermostat runs our home heating and cooling system, the body's hypothalamus, a tiny organ in the brain, senses body temperature. Venturing out on the hot side of the comfort zone? Warm blood from the inner core of the body is diverted by the hypothalamus in a wondrous manner that closes certain blood vessels and opens others nearer the surface of the skin, where excess heat can be radiated away.

Of course, the action of the hypothalamus in activating the sweat glands to return you to the comfort zone is no surprise, but did you know *why*? When perspiration evaporates from the surface of the skin, heat is removed. Thus, sweating is a process that lowers body temperature. Moisten a portion of your hand, then blow on it—as the moisture evaporates, the skin is cooled.

Is your hypothalamus getting the signal that you're dropping into the colder area of the comfort zone? No problem. Blood nearer the surface of the body is shunted inward to the core to conserve heat, and your muscles are set into rapid, small contractions to generate yet more heat. You call it shivering!

The Thermostat That Sets Your Fat

Perhaps the most amazing thermostat in our bodies has been uncovered in recent obesity research. We appear to have developed "set points" for body fat, a degree of body fatness that our bodies literally grow comfortable with. In as yet unknown ways, our bodies can sense and adjust both the rate at which we burn calories at rest (the "basal metabolic rate") and the amount we eat. Early in our lives, this stubborn fat thermostat is set by our levels of physical activity, our general eating habits, and genetic determinants. When we attempt to lose body fat solely through dietary means (eating fewer calories), our thermostat literally reduces the number of calories burned through basal metabolism. A drop of five hundred calories a day in intake will be met by a corresponding drop in calories burned at rest. The net result? You're eating less, but burning less, and the body fat still taunts you.

Amazingly, when you *gain* small amounts of fat, or simply turn *up* your caloric intake for several days, the body responds by turning up the thermostat, and the basal metabolic rate rises. You're eating more, but burning more—and your weight remains fairly stable.

Fortunately, for those of us wishing to change the setting of our thermostat, it *can* be done. Exercise is the key. Exercising enough to burn off an additional two hundred calories a day can effect a resetting of the thermostat and start the fat-loss process. When combined with dietary restriction (also as moderate as two hundred calories a day), long-term fat loss can be achieved.

Our Psychological Thermostat

Why this lengthy digression into feedback and thermostat? Because our self-image is very definitely a thermostat, keeping us in a psychological comfort zone. Our "set point" for winning is arrived at over time, based on belief in ourselves, our abilities, and our worth.

With a strong and healthy belief in ourselves and what we are capable of, we can go out and survive the stress of day-to-day living and reaching worthy goals. When our comfort zone is set at "high," we believe we can handle whatever is thrown at us. If we dare venture beyond our safety zone, we pull back. The risks are too great for who we think we are. If our efforts to win fall below the comfort zone, we feed back to our self-image some positive self-talk: "Next time, I'll do better"; "I *can* do that"; "Harder work and better concentration will win me that prize."

With a low self-image, however, our psychological thermostat is set correspondingly low. Not believing that he or she is capable of much or worth much, the low-image loser is comfortable with failure. When challenged to venture out on the high side or take a chance to change the status quo, he or she pulls back. "I'm not capable of that; that's beyond my meager abilities. It's not worth the effort. Why bother?" goes the negative self-talk.

At my seminars, I like to check a person's self-esteem when he or she first enters the meeting room. In this way, I determine the awareness and needs of my audience.

A woman came into the seminar room and sat down next to my wife, Susan, in the first row.

As she sat down, I said, "Good morning, are you attending the seminar alone?"

She answered, "No, I'm divorced!"

"How long have you been single?" I asked, trying to sound nonjudgmental.

She replied, "I've been divorced for two years now."

I asked another question: "Are the divorce proceedings still going on?"

She looked puzzled. "Why no, of course not. I told you it happened two years ago!"

I smiled reassuringly. "Well, then, if you were divorced two years ago, you are single *now*."

What that lady learned during the seminar took me thirty-five years of self-doubt to figure out. And that is, you never carry mistakes, childhood labels, or failure forward. You don't wear failure like a coat. The performer is always valuable, while the performances are learning experiences, not to be repeated if negative and to be reinforced constantly if positive.

Now, when new friends or associates ask our seminar graduate, "Are you married?" she answers, unhesitatingly, "No, I am not married." She is a powerful demonstration of the truth that we are what we see, what we do, and—most important—*what we think.*

When we look in a mirror, there are three reflections: the child of our past, the person we are today, and the person we will become. We can never totally erase experiences from our memories. If they were negative, our thermostats may be set at win-lose or even no-win. But we can reset our thermostats. With the right role models and the right self-talk, we can change the perceptions that have twisted and colored our image of who we really are. In the next two chapters, we'll look further at how to reset our self-esteem thermostats at win-win.

LOSERS	WINNERS	DOUBLE WINNERS
See a problem in every solution	Seek a solution in every problem	Help others solve their problem

5

Turning Your Self-Image Thermostat to Win-Win

A good way to determine how you feel about yourself is to check the way you feel about your body. How do you treat it? What is your life-style?

I used to look at my body much as someone views his second car—an older clunker that was good for transportation. Mine was a 1933 model, with a half-inflated spare tire and a carburetor running with a little too much cholesterol in the fuel lines. I figured my "1933 Waitley" would get me from birth to death, with maybe an occasional tune-up and, if things got really bad, a valve job.

For fuel, I used bean burritos, french fries, banana moon pies, Twinkies, Milk Duds, and strawberry shakes. I never thought about trying unleaded or premium stuff. After all, it was only something to run on and the environment was so polluted anyway.

I had been traveling the lecture circuit every day for the past year and had come back from my latest trip totally exhausted. Here I was, a so-called specialist in high self-esteem and winning behavior, and my own life was anything but together. To put it another way, I was falling apart.

I Tried the Grocery Bag Test

I had a few days off before my next tour and, while going through the mail, I came upon a flyer advertising a "Healthy

Human Behavior" seminar. It was being offered in a nearby town—only thirty minutes away.

I'll go incognito, I thought. Maybe I'll learn something before going back on the road.

After a rousing lecture on the evils of junk food and the need for exercise, the facilitator closed the session with instructions on how to take the "Self-Image Test" in the privacy of our own homes. The next evening, while Susan and the children were cleaning up the dinner dishes, I slipped away to the bedroom and turned the lock. Following the "Healthy Human Behavior" instructor's orders to the letter, I pulled the drapes and removed all my clothing. Next, I took a large paper bag, cut out two eyeholes, and put it over my head. Wearing only my grocery bag, I marched over to the full-length mirror to begin the "Self-Image Test."

I stared through the holes in the bag and monitored my response to the sight that greeted me. Why was I overwhelmed by the desire to laugh and cry at the same time? Who was this naked stranger? A chubby prowler turned exhibitionist? Some itinerant streaker who had gotten lost on the way to Weight Watchers?

I Saw Miss Piggy in the Rearview Mirror

Old Gray Eyes, the man I had come to know, understand, excuse, and adore, was gone. With the bag over my head, I had to concentrate on my sags, bulges, and creases objectively, for the first time in a long while. I gave my flabby body a Miss America quarter turn to the right and almost dialed 911, our local emergency number. "It's incredible how certain angles can make you look so wide," I muttered, as I pinched well over an inch on one of my love handles.

Shaken, but still determined to complete the test, I did what the instructor had said was reserved for those people with very high self-esteem. I turned completely around for a total rear view in the nude and saw Miss Piggy twice!

"I don't know who you are," I said aloud, "but I wish you'd get dressed and leave."

Just then, out of my grocery-bag eyehole, I noticed that Susan, my loving wife, had tiptoed in and had been observing me, pinching and muttering with a grocery bag over my head. The door had not locked after all!

Susan shook her head and made one of her usual practical observations: "It's finally happened, hasn't it? Denis, you've been on too many airplanes and changed time zones too many times in one month. Have you thought about settling down and taking a teaching job at the university?"

"It's not what you think," I said quickly. "I'm running an experiment."

"You aren't in one of those new cult movements, are you? With all the airports you're in, you didn't buy some book from one of those weird people, did you?"

I had to think fast. After all, I was a distinguished Ph.D. My wife respected me—at least up until now. It was late October; maybe I could joke my way out of this with a little seasonal humor:

"Trick or treat, dear. What do you think?"

Susan pursed her lips and said, "I think I'll take the trick. Look, be kind to yourself. If you're going to streak our bedroom in this condition, don't cut eyeholes in the bag. You'll like what you see better."

I knew the jig was up, so I decided to unbag and make the best of it. I told her about the seminar, the Self-Image Test, and my growing awareness of feeling "a little out of control."

"I think you're right," Susan agreed. "Our medicine cabinet has too many pills. The fridge is full of too much junk food—especially your bulk shipment of banana moon pies."

"Yes, and I noticed the garage when I drove in tonight," I said. "It doesn't need cleaning; it needs a bulldozer. Even the car is cluttered. I've got to stop and get my life in order."

"Well," Susan mused, "I've been trying to feed you more fruit, but the only flavor you seem to like is banana in you-know-what. If you want to reform, count on me to help."

Why Treat a Ferrari Like a Junk Heap?

And "reform" I did—not a complete turnaround but a significant change of direction. My diet is radically improved, much less junky. Some of the bulges are gone and I'm working on others. The bag experiment, ridiculous as it had seemed, had done its job. I saw what that instructor had wanted me to see. You can live with an external view, from the outside in, and let your environment and circumstances control you. Or, you can live from the inside out and take charge. And what better place to start with than your body—the most marvelous machine you'll ever operate. Why treat a Ferrari like a broken-down pickup? Why use a thoroughbred to pull a plow?

Environment is but a looking glass that will quickly tell you if you are living from the outside in or the inside out. When you look in the mirror, clothed or nude, bagged or not, it can be the moment of truth, *if you take the time to look closely and ask some tough questions:*

Am I looking at someone I respect?
Am I going where I want to go in life?
Am I doing what I want to do?
Am I becoming what I want to become?
Do I see someone I really want to be?
Can I share my values and knowledge with others without apology or embarrassment?
Does my life purpose benefit others as well as myself?
Am I planting shade trees under which I may never sit?

If you can answer an unequivocal *yes* to at least seven out of the nine questions above, your self-esteem should be in pretty good shape. If you have to answer *sometimes* or *no* to at least five or six of these questions, your self-esteem thermostat needs turning up.

We aren't born with self-esteem. As with every other feeling, we learn to like ourselves through practice. And much as the practice of any skill must be structured carefully to maximize learning, so must the process through which self-esteem is built be scrutinized and understood.

There are various systems for looking at self-image. One I have found most helpful gives us four different dials to check on our self-esteem thermostat:

- a sense of belonging
- a sense of identification
- a sense of worthiness
- a sense of control

We'll look at belonging, identification, and worthiness in this chapter. We'll spend most of chapter 6 on control.

Belonging—Our Affiliation Drive

We have perhaps no deeper-seated need than to feel we are part of something larger than ourselves. This is our sense of *belonging;* that is, being wanted, accepted, enjoyed, and loved by ones dear to us. Everyone has a strong desire to belong to, or be a part of, someone or something—what the psychologists call an "affiliation drive." This need encompasses people, places, and things.

Our need to belong is first satisfied when our parents make us feel important to them. We come to learn that, as members of the family unit, we have rights which will be respected. Our opinions can be expressed in an open manner, and they will be met with warmth, understanding, and acceptance. It is most important that children enjoy this kind of relationship with parents, but that is only a beginning. Other family members, relatives, friends, and teachers all play a vital role in helping children feel accepted and loved as they learn to belong.

As we move into adulthood, the need to belong doesn't diminish. In many of us, it may increase, depending on how we were treated when younger. And make no mistake, we *all* have this thing called an "affiliation drive." No one is too big, strong, talented, or tough to go without acceptance from others.

Jackie Robinson made history in 1947 when he became the first black baseball player to break into the major leagues by joining the Brooklyn Dodgers. Branch Rickey, owner of the Dodgers at that time, told Robinson, "It'll be tough. You're going to take abuse you never dreamed of. But if you're willing to try it, I'll back you all the way."

And Rickey was right. Jackie was abused verbally (not to mention physically by runners coming into second base). Racial slurs from the crowd and members of his own team, as well as the opponents, were standard fare. One day, Robinson was having it particularly tough. He had booted two ground balls and the boos were cascading over the diamond. In full view of thousands of spectators, Pee Wee Reese, the immortal Dodger shortstop, walked over and put his arm around Jackie Robinson, major league baseball's first black ball player, right in the middle of the game.

"That may have saved my career," Robinson reflected later. "Pee Wee made me feel like I belonged."[1]

A sense of belonging—how vital to us all! Do you recall the times when a new kid came to school and didn't seem to "fit in"? Do you remember when the rest of the kids, especially the class bullies, used the poor newcomer to pump up their diminished self-esteem by persecuting the kid? Maybe you're like me and even remember being that kid!

It doesn't get any easier when you grow up. Being a new kid on the block (the new secretary, salesman, computer programmer, etc.) is never easy. Being the new neighbors in the cul-de-sac, or the new couple at church or at the club, is always a bit stiff and uncomfortable. For all of us, acceptance by our peers, our neighbors, and our colleagues is a real win. If you don't believe it, try to go without acceptance from others for very long and notice what it does to your confidence, performance, and general feelings of self-esteem.

Remember Tandem Computer, the Camelot-like firm described in chapter 2? Tandem practices the Double Win in many ways, not the least of which is the personal welcome every new employee gets from Jim Treybig, Tandem's chief executive officer. Treybig makes it a point to personally appear at orientation sessions for new employees to welcome each one and explain the company's philosophies. So personable is Treybig in making people feel they belong that he's considered bigger than life by everyone at Tandem. One employee says: "Jimmy is really a symbol here. He's a sign that every person here is a human being. He tries to make you feel part of the organization from the first day you are here. That's something people talk about."[2]

Example after example can be taken from other "best run" companies across America. The 99.5 percent service level of the Frito-Lay sales force is another example. At Frito-Lay, legends of a sort have grown up around stories of ten thousand potato chip salesmen ". . . slogging through sleet, mud, hail, snow, and rain."[3] These people aren't delivering mail; they are working with fierce pride to uphold a service level that some efficiency experts would call unreasonable or overkill.

But Frito-Lay's 99.5 percent service level is neither extravagant nor foolish. In fact, it is a Double Win maneuver that results in double benefit: Frito-Lay salesmen feel they belong to a tremendous organization of which they can be proud. Frito-Lay customers (whether it's a mom-and-pop store in the boondocks or a big supermarket in a suburban mall) feel they belong to an exclusive family that gets treated in a very special way.

You may be familiar with a little book called *The One-Minute Manager*, which spent twelve months on *The New York Times* bestseller list in 1983 and 1984. You don't read too far into this little manual on management to learn that building self-esteem, especially a sense of belonging, is a key principle of the book. Three basic principles managers can learn from *The One-Minute Manager* are to help employees set goals and to follow up on these employees, if only briefly; to praise them when they do something right; and correct them quickly if they are getting off course.[4]

Can You Make Yourself Feel You Belong?

A lot of people in this win-lose world feel they don't belong. You could well be one of them. What can you do if you aren't feeling that accepted in your family, your church, or your place of work? Here are two ideas:

Include, don't exclude. A lot of people who feel they don't belong are causing a certain amount of their alienation themselves. They don't try to include others and, therefore, they feel excluded as well. No matter how excluded you might feel, chances are you can find someone else in the group who is being left out, too. Watch any clique operate and you will soon detect an almost blatant kind of "smuggery." It is all so easy to become "in" with a group and then sit back and say, "I paid my dues and I am set. I earned it—let the other guy do the same."

I have always admired the innocence of children and their willingness to "tell it like it is." A friend of mine has a most adorable daughter who once came home and told her mother that she and her peers had formed a club. Mama showed great interest and asked who was included. The little girl reported, "Everyone but Barbara Smith."

"Well," said her mother, "don't you think you ought to invite Barbara to join?"

"Oh, no, we *can't,*" replied the daughter. "The name of this club is the 'I Hate Barbara Smith Club'!"

The child, who was basically a good and gentle person, was merely reflecting a very human tendency—to "earn" one's way into a certain part of society and then maintain the value of one's membership by excluding equally deserving others.

So, if you've tried a new environment or taken some other risk that places you in a new situation, look around for those who may feel more excluded than you do. Try to make them "feel like they belong." You will both be the better for it—a Double Win indeed!

Seek to make a contribution. One of the obvious ways to feel part of any group is to try to help or contribute to that group's cause or well-being. Teenagers often complain about feeling they "don't belong" at home anymore. I often feel like asking them how much they are contributing to the home front. It is not really so surprising that fifty to one hundred years ago, when most families were together in a farm setting, the children did not have as many problems with feeling accepted and loved by Mom and Dad because they were constantly working and contributing to the family welfare. On a farm, everybody has work to do. Today we have moved to the cities and the suburbs. We are "blessed" with all kinds of laborsaving devices, and so many activities, teams, and organizations for everyone to become part of, that the family is torn in a dozen directions. Children often complain they don't feel part of things and the reason is obvious. They have very little to do. "Chores" are assigned, true, but many of these are often token tasks that are invented to give a child "training." The absolute "do or die" necessity for everyone to pitch in, in order to help the family survive, is no longer a fact in most homes today, and I believe we are double losers for it.

In chapter 3, we discussed the principle of synergism, where the whole becomes greater than the sum of its parts. Often, synergism occurs when different people start contributing to one another. A vivid example of how all this can happen is a story that came out of one of New York City's boroughs. A group of adult volunteers works with handicapped teenagers at the Queens Botanical Garden to give the youngsters instruction and practice in horticulture while helping them develop job skills. Many of these adults are elderly, the kind of people who often feel useless and as if they don't belong anywhere. But everyone feels that he or she belongs in this setting. Staff members at the Botanical Garden teach the adult volunteers and the children basic plant care, greenhouse maintenance, plant propagation, and tool safety. Everyone learns together in an effort financed by a state funding agency.

Students, handicapped kids thirteen to nineteen years old, on release time from work-study programs in their schools, do the physical work. The adult volunteers provide direction and guidance.

Here is a situation where everybody wins. The students get a chance to learn good work habits, gain self-esteem from useful work, and learn skills that may enable them to become independent. The elderly volunteers have the joy of working with young people and feeling useful and needed as well. The Queens Botanical Garden staff members have the joy of knowing they are helping the older folks, as well as the young ones, which adds even more value to the beauties of the Garden, which it is their pleasure to tend.[5]

This program is one of the most rewarding forms of the Double Win: a profusion of exploding chain-reaction wins that arises from mutually satisfying efforts.

Identification Asks Us Three Crucial Questions

The next dial on our self-image thermostat deals with our sense of identification. Here we find three crucial questions waiting to be answered:

Who am I?
What am I?
Why am I?

The question "Who am I?" deals with my person, my heritage, my family affiliations. Denis Waitley would answer the question "Who am I?" by saying something like this:

"I am a graying, fifty-one-year-old father of six, married to Susan, six feet even, and weighing 185 lbs. [standard banana moon pie scale]. I comb my hair forward with a blow dryer to cover the thin spots. I'm a combination of English-Welsh and Scotch-Bolivian. [It seems my grandfather was a Welsh Scotsman who married a fiery little Bolivian señorita.] And last of all, as one who spells 'Waitley' with an l-e-y, I am directly related to everyone else in the country with that particular spelling of the name. There are other families who pronounce their name the same, but spell it differently [Waitly or Whately, etc.], but they may or may not be related. All the Waitleys, however, are from one big family."

"What am I?" is a question that deals more with the things I can do or the things I am known for. Again, Denis Waitley would answer this question by saying:

"I'm a psychologist/lecturer who struggles from time to time to learn to be a writer. I'm a former navy carrier jet pilot who now flies private planes from time to time, on a clear day when he can keep the landing field in sight. I'm a counselor who's had opportunity to talk to Super Bowl and Olympic athletes, as well as Apollo Moon Program astronauts, returned Vietnam POWs, and the Iranian hostages. I'm also a good fisherman, a cautious snorkler, a rusty golfer [I don't get out much anymore because it takes too long], and an absolute terror [to my partner] in tennis doubles."

When anyone answers the "What am I?" question, he is dealing with his perception of what he has done, can do, or wishes he could do. Joining me on the lecture circuit at least once a month is Joe Girard, who answers the "What am I?" question by saying, "The best car/truck salesman in the world." Joe could also answer that same question by saying, "A speaker who gets attention and holds it." On many occasions I have watched as Joe has literally *stood upon* the speaker's podium to address the audience. Note, I said he stands *on* the podium, not behind it. As he towers over ten feet in the air, believe me, he does command attention!

And how does Joe command the modest claim of best car/truck salesman in the world? By sending out over thirteen thousand cards *every month* to his customers or would-be customers. Joe believes that a sale really begins *after* the sale, not before. Every month

throughout the year, a customer gets a different letter with an envelope of a different size and color. Inside, the card reads, "I like
you, Happy New Year from Joe Girard." If he sends one in February, it says "Happy George Washington's Birthday."

Are Joe Girard's thirteen thousand cards a month just a gimmick?
The authors of *In Search of Excellence* don't think so. They write:

> But like the top companies, Joe seems genuinely *to care.* Said Joe,
> "The great restaurants in the country have loving care coming out
> of their kitchens . . . and when I sell a car, my customer's gonna
> leave with the same feeling that he'll get when he walks out of a
> great restuarant." Joe Girard sees every customer as an individual.
> When a customer comes back for sevice, Joe fights to get him the
> best. No customer is ever an interruption or a pain in the neck to
> Joe Girard.[6]

Many companies strive to help their sales forces feel every bit as
good about "What am I?" as Joe Girard. Tupperware is one such
corporation. Tupperware management's major task is to keep
eighty thousand salespeople motivated, and they do it with what
they call the "Rally," which is held every Monday night with different groups across the country. Everyone in a sales group gets to
march up in front to share what he or she has done that week. If she
did anything at all, she gets a pin or a badge, possibly several. The
Tupperware Rally is, in fact, a kind of head-to-head competition
because everybody has to share what she did and, naturally, some
have done better than others each week. Nonetheless, it has a positive tone and everybody wins, as the applause and the hoopla and
the pins are distributed liberally among everyone present.

And the Tupperware system works. I have seen it myself when
I've been a guest speaker at the national Tupperware seminars. The
same Rally approach is used in the national seminars and everybody gets excited. Everyone comes out of a Tupperware meeting of
this kind saying, "What am I? I'm a Tupperware salesperson and
I'm really good."

It's not hard to see Double Win principles in Joe Girard's operation, as well as Tupperware's. Girard really cares; he's not just interested in customers and sales, per se. Tupperware encourages
competition, but it's the kind that encourages and enables everyone
to win, not just a few of the "top dogs."[7]

"Why am I?" is the hardest question to answer. Here is where we define ourselves in relationship to our beliefs, ideals, motives, and goals. Here is where we find out if we are hedonistic, living only to have personal pleasure and a good time, or if we are benevolent and caring, existing to help others as well as ourselves. All of us have our own reasons and purposes for existence, whether or not we have defined them. All this is related to our sense of worthiness, which we'll be discussing next.

Unfortunately, however, many people can't answer a question like, "Why am I?" and these people almost always suffer from a lack of self-esteem. My inner approval of myself lasts only as long as I continue to live by my own values and convictions.

So, if Denis Waitley answered the question "Why am I?" he would say:

> "I was created by God to understand the win-win relationships in the world and how to use them to improve the lives of all living things and persons with whom I come in contact. I am here to learn as much as I can, to experience as much as I can, to give as much as I can, to serve my fellow men and women as much as I can, and to love my family as much as I can—as honestly, joyfully, and for as long as I can."

Another way for a would-be Double Winner to answer the question "Why am I?" would be Hans Selye's version of the Golden Rule, already mentioned under the Profile of a Double Winner in chapter 3: "Earn Thy Neighbor's Love."

A sense of wanting to serve your fellow man is essential. Perhaps no one could answer questions like "What am I?" and "Why am I?" better than Antonio Stradivari, the Italian violin maker, who lived from 1644 to 1737. Stradivari died at the age of ninety-three, during a time when the average life expectancy was a little over thirty years. His tools were primitive. He taught himself his trade and he usually worked alone, until late in life when his sons joined him in business.

Stradivari put the best of himself into his profession. When he was finished with an instrument and was certain that his craftsmanship measured up to his own personal standards, he would sign his name on the violin. Today, nearly 250 years later, a genuine

Stradivarius violin sells for thousands of dollars and the name Stradivarius is a household word around the world.

Almost everyone has heard the name Stradivarius (which is the Latin pronunciation). While this violin maker's name is known everywhere, throughout history there have been many individuals with uncommon standards of excellence, but little notoriety. And today, in industry, the arts, and the sciences, there are thousands of men and women, unknown and unsung, who simply refuse to turn out shoddy work. They are in the minority, but then they always have been. Remember, the win-lose ethic is the natural way. The win-win ethic is the unnatural—but oh, so worthwhile—approach.

A respect for quality is the mark of high self-esteem. People who consistently do things well set their own high standards to which they make themselves measure up. In so doing, they create a Double Win:

1. They give the best of themselves to benefit others and their work is a source of joy and satisfaction, while they experience deep self-respect from being uncommon contributors.
2. They build the kind of security that lasts a lifetime or beyond, because respect for quality always endures and will always command the highest price.

Or to put it all in one brief sentence: If you are willing to identify with excellence and put your name on your work, both your work and your name will stand the test of time.

And now it's time for you to answer the big three: Who are you? What are you? Why are you? Take your time and give yourself lots of support and approval for being unique and special. Answer every question on the positive side (don't use negative programming, given to you by misguided or unskilled parents, teachers, employers, friends, etc.). You may not be Antonio Stradivari, but you *are* good—at something.

As for why you are here, that may take some time. What are your values and goals? What is your life purpose? Double Winners know the answer to this question, or at least they are always working on refining that answer.

Worthiness Asks, "Do I Really Like Myself?"

The third gauge on the self-image thermostat is a sense of worthiness. It is related, in part, to our sense of belonging and our sense of identification because we need to feel accepted and acknowledged by others, in order to confirm our attitudes toward ourselves. Deeper than that, however, our sense of worthiness depends upon our own self-approval. Others may accept us and make us feel we belong; others may be lavish in their praise of who, what, and why we are, but if we have violated our own conscience or sense of values, we will not feel very worthy. I believe one's sense of worthiness especially suffers in win-lose situations and relationships. Fortunately, one's sense of worthiness probably takes no greater beating than in the public-school classroom. All of us can remember win-lose situations where our sense of worth definitely came out second-best, due to not knowing the answer, getting a bad grade, or just feeling stupid because of the way the teacher and/or our classmates treated us.

There is an oft-repeated tale about a new teacher who went to a Navajo Indian reservation. Bill couldn't figure it out. Nothing he'd studied in his educational course helped, and he certainly hadn't seen anything like it in his student-teaching days back in Phoenix, Arizona. What would happen, almost daily, went something like this: He would call five of the young Navajo students to the chalkboard to put up a simple math problem from their homework. There they all stood, silently, without movement, unwilling to report their results.

Could I have chosen five students who couldn't do the problem? Bill thought. *No, it couldn't be that.* And so he finally asked the students what was wrong. And in their answer, he got a surprising lesson about self-image and a sense of worthiness from his young Indian pupils.

It seemed that the students respected each other's individuality and the fact that not all of them were capable of doing the problems. Even at their early age, they understood the senselessness of the win-lose approach in the classroom. They believed *no one* would win if any students were "shown up" or embarrassed at the chalkboard. So, they refused to compete with each other in public. Once he understood, Bill had no problem. He changed the system so he could check each child's problems individually, but not at any child's expense in front of his classmates. They all wanted to learn—but not at someone else's expense.

This little story from a Navajo Indian reservation is a great example of how the sense of worthiness can work. The student who wouldn't show up less-able classmates didn't violate their sense of self-respect. And classmates who were supported (not embarrassed) also had their sense of worthiness nurtured and strengthened. And, in showing the wisdom to not force his Navajo pupils to do something that violated their own code, the young teacher, Bill, also improved his sense of worthiness.

This principle of "feeling worthy" and "making others feel worthy also" is one of the basic goals that I see across the land as corporations everywhere pursue their search for excellence. For example, Leonard Abramson, chief executive officer of United States Health Care Systems, Inc., says: "Building something from your own idea is the best possible way to live. The inner applause you give yourself when you succeed outweighs anything anyone else could ever give you."[8]

Vic Barouh is another executive who understands the power and importance of a sense of self-worth—for himself as well as his employees. Barouh, fifty-seven, is the founder, chairman, and majority stockholder of Barouh-Eaton Allen Corp., usually called Ko-Rec-Type, after its best-known consumer product. Barouh is a man known for building a profitable company by "doing everything wrong." One employee, who spent twenty years with a competitor before joining Barouh's team, says, "If you judge it by the way the book says you're supposed to do things, this place shouldn't work."[9]

And what does Barouh, whose growing company has international sales of more than $50 million, do that is so unorthodox?

A business interested in controlling costs shouldn't hire people it doesn't have jobs for, or tie up its cash in interest-free loans to employees. . . . A company in a highly competitive industry should not dispatch a former stenographer to open a new branch plant. Its chairman should not load pallets. He should not kiss the women who work for him. He should not call them girls. He should not shout so much. He should not be so naive as to believe that love and respect are crucial to business success.[10]

Barouh, of course, does all these unlikely things and more. The result? His employees love him. One says, "There are people here who would die for Vic Barouh."

Barouh's Double Win approach to building self-worth in his people includes his style of dealing with employees who make mistakes:

> "When I want something done and I express anger and hate to someone because they didn't do it right, I will solve the problem for that day, but the very next day I've got the very same problem again. . . .

> "But when you approach them and say, 'Guys, we made a mistake. It's a costly mistake, and we can't take that costly mistake, because if it repeats itself again then I'm out of business. I don't have a job anymore. If I don't have a job, you don't have a job. And I'm gonna tell you something else. I'm not theatening, you, 'cause I need you to make it right. I can't be all over, so I need you to take care of your end.' "[11]

Barouh probably has never read *The One-Minute Manager,* but his style is the same. He knows how to praise and how to reprimand and still keep the employees' self-worth intact.

People who build a good sense of worthiness in themselves and others are people who understand and believe in personal values. If you were fortunate enough to have parents who taught you the importance of responsibility, honesty, initiative, love, joy, courage, faith, self-control, and persistence, be sure to utter a prayer of thanks once or twice a day. If you weren't that fortunate, you can still build your own values base by asking yourself some of the right questions:

Is my emphasis on following specific rules that may or may not be relevant?

Is the exterior of my life-style more important to me than the interior?

Is making a good impression on others more important than being true to myself?

Am I basing my code of conduct on time-tested principles that still apply in today's society?

Proper and worthwhile values that are clearly understood will give anyone the ability to establish a true sense of self-worth. And once we have established a good sense of worthiness, we can handle criticism or praise in the right way. But without this sense of worthiness, we become defensive to criticism and paranoid about praise, always thinking the other person has ulterior motives.

Individuals with good self-esteem can accept or reject the opinions of others, but never depend upon them for their sense of worthiness. For such individuals, a sense of worthiness is a permanent and integral part of their self-concept. What others think of them does not influence their sense of worthiness. The key factor is what they think of themselves.

Still to Come: Central Control

So far we have checked three of the four dials on our self-image thermostat.

The reading on our sense of belonging is important because we all have an "affiliation drive" that creates a deep-seated need to feel a part of someone or something that is important to us.

The reading on our sense of identification is even more important because we all need to answer the three big questions of life:

"Who am I?"
"What am I?"
"Why am I?"

The reading on our sense of worthiness is probaby most important, however, because this dial tells us whether or not we like ourselves. If you can't applaud yourself from within, it won't matter that much if you're getting applauded from without. You either won't believe the applause or you will discount it. In effect, you won't hear the applause because the negative inner messages will be holding all of your attention.

One other dial remains to make the settings on our self-image thermostat complete. It can have tremendous effect on the other three dials—perhaps it is the real central control of personal self-esteem. We will look at this all-important dial—a sense of control or competency—in the next chapter.

LOSERS	WINNERS	DOUBLE WINNERS
Fix the blame	Fix the situation	Fix what caused the problem

Control: Cornerstone of a High Self-Image

You may have seen the TV commercial for a well-known hair product, which depicts a handsome hero and his frightened lady friend in the cockpit of a plane in a steep power dive. Our perfectly groomed hero is at the controls and calmly saying:

"Four thousand feet . . . three thousand feet . . . two thousand feet . . . but I'm under control!"

While the psychology of this commercial is designed to sell hair-dressing, it teaches a valuable lesson about self-esteem. The fourth and in many ways most important dial on our self-image thermostat is a sense of control. When I feel "in control," I feel competent and able to perform in a manner necessary to reach my goals. A sense of control assures me I have the strength to face life's problems with adequacy, courage, and hope. This confidence in myself is built upon a foundation of experiencing success. When anyone begins anything new, he or she usually has little confidence because of the lack of experiencing any success. This is true when learning to ride a bicycle, ski, figure-skate, fly a high-performance jet aircraft, or lead people. Success breeds success. As we noted in chapter 3, the follower of the Double Win philosophy focuses on past successes and forgets past failures. The Double Winner uses errors and mistakes as a way to learn, but then dismisses them from his or her mind.

The person with a poor self-image, however, destroys self-confidence by remembering past failures and forgetting any past successes. Not only does he remember the failures; he etches them into his mind with feelings of guilt and condemnation.

It's not hard to see that the "dwelling on failure" mentality not only erodes any feelings one might have of getting a sense of control; it also chisels away at your sense of worthiness, identification, and belonging:

> "I blew it again [with the sale, with the dinner party, with disciplining my son, etc., etc.]. Nothing seems to work. I set goals and never reach them. I'm a lousy performer. It's no wonder I'm not really accepted [in my company, family, church, etc.]."

If you want to win—and especially if you want to practice the Double Win—you have to settle one thing right now. It doesn't matter how many times you have failed in the past. What matters is carving out tiny footholds of success and remembering, reinforcing, and dwelling upon those footholds.

She Lost Leg and Gained Self-Esteem

Carol Schuller, daughter of my friend Dr. Robert Schuller, pastor of the Crystal Cathedral in Garden Grove, California, knows something about concentrating on successes while forgetting the failures. When she was thirteen, she went for a ride on the back of a motorcycle, which wound up in a head-on collision with a car. Carol landed eighty-six feet away, with a shattered leg that had to be removed just below the knee.

When Bob Schuller heard about the accident (he was on a trip to Korea at the time), he had to go into an airport rest room to weep and pray. He came out with a feeling of peace, and realized the accident had to have happened for a reason.

But Carol had to find the reason, and she did, with the help of a friend who introduced her to snow skiing after nearly two years of convalescing. A natural athlete, Carol caught on quickly to using outriggers, smaller skis attached to the end of her ski poles. She skis on one leg and does not use her prosthesis, which "just gets in the way." Before the age of sixteen she had placed third in her first skiing race, and during the 1984 skiing season she competed in the national championship for handicapped athletes, where she finished second in the downhill, third in the slalom and giant slalom, and took second place overall.

Already clocked at top speeds over seventy miles per hour, Carol has a rigorous training schedule that includes swimming, aerobics, and weights, plus several hours of skiing each day. Does she feel handicapped? On the contrary, she believes that many people may feel sorry for a person with a physical handicap, but those same people are often actually worse off, due to one reason or another.

Is she simply trying to please her father by upholding his "possibility thinking" teachings? Carol doesn't think so. The loss of her leg doesn't bother her that much, and she says: "Before my accident, I was pretty athletic, so I just didn't let myself think that the accident would change anything."

Carol Schuller isn't dwelling on her past failures and tragedies. She is focusing on her present successes and the goal to someday enter world-class international competition.

"Going down the hill doesn't make you feel handicapped," she says. "You can be out among people; there's no holding you back. You can do anything anybody else can do and more. Not because you're handicapped, but because you're really good."[1]

"You Have to Make the Most of It"

Carol Schuller is a striking example of someone who has maintained her self-esteem by achievement in the face of great odds. Everyone needs to experience a high level of achievement in some area of his or her life, appropriate to his or her age, abilities, and limitations. When developing a sense of control or competence, you have to take into account your abilities and your weaknesses and keep a realistic balance between the two as you develop new expectations.

Another story from the ski slopes vividly portrays how all this can happen. In Jimmy Heuga's case, however, he didn't learn to ski as a teenager after losing a leg. Heuga had been on skis since age two, and had finished just behind silver-medal winner and good friend Billy Kidd to win the Bronze in the slalom at the 1964 Olympic Games at Innsbruck. But even while the crowds cheered Heuga's achievement, the dread effects of multiple sclerosis were already taking their toll in his body. In all too short a time, he was reduced to life in a wheelchair and was told he would never walk—much less ski—again.

Jimmy could have dwelt on failure and tragedy, but he chose to seek success and regain control of his life. He sought therapy to help his limp limbs, but no doctors would give him any. It seems the AMA had long since determined that until some new drug or other treatment could be discovered, total immobilization was the best chance to prolong a patient's life. But Heuga wouldn't listen, and began swimming and other therapy. He took tiny steps of success and forgot the failures and the so-called danger. One neurologist told him, "I hear you and I see you as living proof, but this is just against everything we've been teaching."

Heuga fought his way back to mobility and decided to take his story on the road. He traveled the country, talking to hospital wards full of MS patients, to bring the good news that they didn't have to let MS ruin their lives. Heuga tells others (as well as himself):

> "What we have to do is think in positive terms; *not* in terms of what we can't do, but in terms of what we are able to do. Because if we think in terms of what we can't do, we can be pretty depressed. If you can knit, knit. If you can play cards, play cards. But don't sit around thinking in negative terms. We all have to make the best of it."

Thanks to Jimmy Heuga, the AMA has now accredited a physical-exercise program for patients suffering from multiple sclerosis. The program was developed by Heuga and his two doctors. Today, Jimmy Heuga is "alive and well," living at Winter Park, Colorado—and ski racing, of course. Billy Kidd lives just over the mountain in Steamboat Springs and they remain good friends. Kidd, in fact, goes through the same daily ritual as his friend Heuga—a cold shower every morning. After MS struck Heuga, he and Kidd had lost contact and, when they met again in the mid-seventies, Kidd was overwhelmed by the way Jimmy had whipped his problem. Jimmy's comment: "You know, Billy, the most difficult thing about having MS is taking one cold shower a day." Heuga had developed a philosophy. If he could get up and take a cold shower in the morning, he knew he could take anything the day had to offer.

"That cold shower is my discipline," says Jimmy. "That's what tells me that I don't ever want to give up on myself."[2]

Control: A Powerful Motivator for Success

Stories like Carol Schuller's and Jimmy Heuga's are dramatic accounts of people who suffered failure and loss but fought back to regain control of their lives, and the high self-esteem to go with it. Less dramatic, but every bit as significant, is the way leading corporations and businesses research and develop the concept of control (competence) in the lives of employees. The smart companies know that if you label a man a loser, he'll start acting like one. Research studies show that the old cliché "Nothing succeeds like success" has a sound scientific basis. How well you are actually doing is not the main issue; it's whether you perceive that you are doing well that counts.

A well-known research experiment had a group of adults solving ten different puzzles. Everyone worked on the same puzzles and turned in their results. Half of the people being tested were told that they had done well and solved at least seven out of the ten puzzles correctly. The other half of the control group learned that they had done poorly, that they had gotten seven out of ten puzzles wrong. The "puzzle results" were fictitious, of course. But the researchers wanted to see what the two groups would do when given ten more puzzles to solve. The results were predictable: Those who had been told they had done well in the first round did better in the second, while those who had been told they had done poorly did worse. "Mere association with past personal success apparently leads to more persistence, higher motivation, or something that makes us do better."[3]

The sense of control so important to your self-image also has a lot to do with the concepts of power and authority. Any employee is concerned about questions like these:

"Am I strong enough or influential enough to do what I'd like to do on this job?"

"Do I have the authority to make the moves I know need to be made to get the job done?"

As I deal with corporations around the world, I see more and more instances where employers are putting more control (power) in the hands of their employees. One glowing example is Celestial Seasonings, a $30 million firm that manufactures herb teas, under the Double Win leadership of Mo Siegel. I'll be telling Mo's story in more detail in chapter 9, but right here, I want to share something he told me on the phone recently that beautifully illustrates the value in giving employees power and control.

At Celestial Seasonings, the production line can turn out four thousand tea bags per minute. If any of the workers see anything at all that might be going wrong, he or she can pull a lever and shut down the entire line on the spot! All the workers are constantly checking product quality, with the goal of reaching a zero-defect level in quality control.

I asked Mo if all this checking for defects slowed things down. He told me that the days Celestial Seasonings gets its highest production levels are the days when quality control is the highest, with the machines consistently putting out a good product. Mo said, "What is thrilling to me is to watch these people, empowered with the ability to shut that line down. They care as much about the quality and the production numbers as I do."

Much the same sort of story is told at Hallmark, where the company printers have refused to print certain cards (even when they've passed the inspection of the design committees) because they're "not Hallmark quality." The point is that, given power, people will assume responsibility for quality.

Self-Control in a Black Porsche

About here, you might be thinking, "Hallmark and Celestial Seasonings sound like great places to work. At my place, about all they let me control is going to the rest room, as long as I don't do it more than twice a day." If your company hasn't caught up with Celestial Seasonings, don't despair. Work on your sense of control by working on yourself. It's amazing how we can so easily subordinate control of our lives to strangers. One good example is on the freeways and tollways that we use to go to work. I confess that back when I was a headstrong young navy jet jockey, I lacked a certain amount of self-control. I used to love to don my black leather Italian racing gloves, slip into the cockpit of my sleek black Porsche, complete with silver racing stripes, and hit the freeways at about seven o'clock in the morning. My mission? To hunt down and intimidate every Volkswagen "Bug" I could find!

On one particular morning, I thought I was in luck. I felt like William Holden in *The Bridges at Toko-Ri*, as he sneaked up on an unsuspecting Mig-15. She was going to work, singing along with the radio, drinking coffee, and chatting with her roommate, all at the same time, while her little VW Bug did forty-five miles per hour in the fast lane!

Now, at that time of my life, if anything could send me into a state of totally hyper and out-of-control, it was a female driver, in her Bug, singing and talking and drinking coffee, while going ten miles per hour under the speed limit in the fast lane. My nostrils flared and the hair on the nape of my neck rose. My heart rate jumped to at least 180 and the adrenaline pumped as I throttled down to keep from stalling out at low speed. I rode her bumper much as I would fly wing in precision-formation flying, and leaned on the horn to let her know she was in my way.

"Move that rolling sewing machine over!" I yelled. She couldn't hear me yell, but she did hear my horn. She waved, smiled in the rearview mirror, and cheerfully slowed down to forty miles per hour, still in the fast lane!

"I'll show you," I snarled. I geared my Porsche down to second and narrowly missed a big Oldsmobile as I pulled over two lanes while digging out my special sign that I had made for use with poky VW Bugs. As I roared up the slow lane doing ninety-five and shaking my fist, I displayed my sign in the driver's window—MOVE IT!

While accomplishing all these maneuvers, I did not see the construction signs up ahead. Work was being done on my lane and it was about to end! Realizing *I* was about to end as well, I hit the brakes and almost caused a multicar pileup as I spun out and wound up in the dirt on the shoulder of the freeway.

There I sat, shaking and fuming, with my Porsche pointed in the wrong direction, while my Bug-flying nemesis rolled on by, still singing along with the radio, still chatting with her roommate, and still drinking her coffee, all at forty-five miles per hour in the fast lane.

Have you ever been out of control to the point where a stranger you'll never see again could ruin your day (not to mention your forever)? My Bug-hunting tale illustrates another facet of this all-important sense of control that we need for good self-esteem. How we control things, and ourselves, is an important aspect of our self-image, because it says so much about how we cope with life. Our competence in these matters involves our sense of power over circumstances, time, responsibilities, usefulness, and the fulfillment of our roles and goals in life. As we fulfill our expectations, we increase our sense of control.

"Imagineering" High Self-Esteem

As we constantly adjust and tinker with the four dials of self-image—belonging, identification, worthiness, and control—we have a powerful tool at our disposal: the practice of positive self-talk. Every waking moment, we can feed our self-image positive thoughts about ourselves and our performances. With practice, we can learn to engage in this kind of self-talk, so relentlessly and vividly, that our self-images will be, in time, molded and modified to conform to new and higher standards.

Walt Disney called this process "Imagineering." It was a word he coined to describe the science/art of putting the imagination to work to create new wonders, new successes, and still newer dreams to fulfill. Every human being is a creator who is capable of using the dual mechanism of self-image and self-esteem to draft winning plans to achieve life's goals.

Our self-image can be directed much like an on-board guidance system in a space-shuttle craft. Directed by such a system, the vehicle seeks the target unerringly. Any slight changes in the environment are compensated for through feedback and mid-course corrections, and the goal is achieved.

The human brain operates similarly to the guidance system in a space shuttle, except that it is far more marvelous and complex than any machine man could ever invent. Simply stated, it works like this:

You set your goal and pursue it.

You monitor feedback as it comes in from the environment (the way people react to your goal seeking, plus the circumstances you encounter).

After receiving feedback, you engage in self-talk. At this point, you have a decision to let that self-talk be positive or negative.

If you choose to program yourself with positive self-talk, the self-
image thermostat in your brain automatically adjusts your
course (if needed) to the right direction.

Without having to consciously think about it anymore, you go on
pursuing, and finally reaching, your goal.

During every moment of our lives, we use our self-talk to program our self-image to work for or against us. The sole function of
the self-image is to follow the instructions given to it, implicitly,
like an obedient computer, reading its disk and responding automatically.

Neuroscientists agree that the human nervous system cannot
distinguish an actual experience from one imagined vividly, emotionally, and in detail. Laboratory experiments have proven that our
attitudes, the way we think, and the way we want to grow (or not
grow) are under our conscious control and become, with practice,
an automatic, unconscious reflex. Winners tell themselves over and
over again, with words, pictures, concepts, and emotions, that they
are winning important personal victories *now*. Double Winners remind themselves how, each time they give of themselves, they receive in return. They never forget that the secret to resetting their
self-image thermostat on win-win is to take responsibility for sharing value with others, rather than gaining power over others.

How Gene Littler Developed That Perfect Swing

Unquestionably, your self-image goes far toward determining
your level of performance. You are usually as successful , or un-
successful, as you expect to be and plan to be. Your self-image
constantly evolves through the performance-based feedback that I
have been calling "self-talk." When you are positive and constructive in your self-talk, your self-image expands and grows to maturity. When you talk down to yourself, you suffer the consequences.

Of course, there's more to winning than using exotic buzz words
like *imagineering* and *self-talk*. No matter how hard we try, no matter
how intensely we visualize, most of us go back to being our "old
selves." We need to develop one more crucial attitude that will help
us develop our self-image to the point where we can make real accomplishments instead of simply engaging in pipe dreams. In sim-

ple terms, this attitude is humility. We must make the decision to learn whatever skills are necessary for success in a chosen area and then pursue that success with constant practice.

For example, in order to be a tennis star, it is not enough to play the "inner game" of tennis, as you let your mind flow free and supposedly let your creative subconscious play for you. While it is true that tennis stars visualize where the next shot will be placed, a few microseconds before their rackets make contact with the ball, nonetheless they have been relentlessly practicing the correct swing of the racket day after day for many years.

The same is true of any sport. I went to La Jolla High School with Gene Littler, the great PGA touring pro, who is generally acknowledged as having the "perfect" golf swing. As teenagers, Gene and I would go to the La Jolla Country Club for practice sessions. Gene would practice while I shagged golf balls. Almost every day, he would hit hundreds of balls to the 60, 75, 100, and 150-yard markers.

As a very young boy, Gene had watched great golfers play. He had taken lessons from a great teaching professional and had learned the correct execution of each shot in the game. The great attitudinal skill that set Gene Littler's self-image thermostat high as a youth was his ability to recognize the effort required and his willingness to pay the price of "practicing winning" on and off the golf course. He knew the saying that applies to every skill, every sport, every business, and every high-performance situation in life:

"You've got to learn the correct swing before you can play the game."

As he mastered the game of golf by observing, imitating, and repeating the correct swings and strokes, he developed a high self-image which, in turn, resulted in a low handicap and an incredible career as a professional. With a self-image built on competency and positive role models, he had a perfect navigational guidance computer during practice and tournament rounds of golf.

When, upon occasion, Gene Littler would hit a bad shot, I would overhear him making corrections with positive self-talk: "That's not like you; keep your head down and follow through." When I saw him hit an outstanding shot, right to the pin, I heard more positive self-talk: "Good, that's more like it. Now we're in the groove!"

Today, Gene Littler lives less than a mile from me. He still has that picture-perfect swing, which he displays on the senior PGA circuit on occasion. He is the most gracious and exemplary professional athlete I have ever known, without a trace of inflated ego and always looking for an opportunity to help someone else win.

How to Keep Your Self-Image Set on Win-Win

It is vital to remember that your self-image is being constantly adjusted by your self-talk. Your self-talk after a performance confirms or denies the self-image setting that you took into that performance. Your own self-talk feedback after every performance is the most critical element in developing an attitude for achieving success. How you respond to a good or bad performance may spell the difference between temporary or fleeting success and a constant, permanent position as a winner. Individuals literally talk themselves out of repeat wins by saying they were very lucky, by discounting their own performance, by attributing the win to external circumstance, by feeling they didn't deserve to win, which signifies guilt, or by becoming so arrogant they fail to continue to practice enough to sustain this same level of performance in the future.

I have observed many sales executives earn much more money in a single month of brilliant performance than they did in the entire previous year. Not able to take the "discomfort" of performing better than their self-image setting, they either take a vacation, stay in the office doing busy work, or misuse their time while in the field. The month following their "record showing" is a disaster. But they think they feel better, because now they are operating more "according to form."

Every now and then, however, I see a salesman who follows one month of brilliant performance by another and another. He has succeeded in resetting his self-image thermostat. He hasn't written off one month of brilliance as a "fluke" or something he "really doesn't deserve." He is using positive self-talk to continue to improve. To be winners, we need to use constructive feedback and self-talk every day. There is nothing magical about positive self-talk. It sounds like this:

"I can."

"I can't wait to start."

"I want to."

"Next time, I'll get it right."
"I'm feeling great about that last effort."
"Thank you, I appreciate your input."
"Let's find a solution to this."

Almost without exception, the real winners, in business, sports, or any other activity in life, have accepted their own uniqueness, feel comfortable with their self-image, and are willing to know and accept them just as they are. And, it's no surprise that such people naturally attract friends and supporters. Winners, especially Double Winners, who give to others from the security of a strong self-image, never stand alone. Confident in who they are and what they are worth, they give unflinchingly and always receive an abundance of enrichment in return.

LOSERS	WINNERS	DOUBLE WINNERS
Let life happen to them	Make life happen for them	Make life a joyous happening for others and themselves

How to Win

We're getting warmed up . . .

Defining and profiling the difference between the win-lose philosophy and the Double Win is basic.

Analyzing the most needed tool for practicing the Double Win—high self-esteem—is crucial.

But just how does one win in life? What do you actually do to be successful in any activity or endeavor?

Success is not something that can be packaged, bottled, or captured in a "simple formula." But there are certain areas and skills you must continue to study and master if you want to live effectively and successfully.

In the next three chapters we will look at nine such skills. They are not a fail-safe formula for instant success, but they will help you learn how to win any race you choose to run. So . . . off with that warm-up suit . . .

Take your marks . . .

Get set

And go!

7

Take Your Marks
(Do You Have a Goal or Just a
Dream?)

Becoming a Double Winner is a lifelong challenge. I'm certainly not where I would like to be yet in practicing the win-win principles. But I am making progress. And I can see and feel a real difference in the quality of the experiences that fit together in the continuing puzzle we call life.

Writing (or reading) any book—particularly a book on "success"—always confronts us with a truth that is so basic we tend to forget it:

Nothing is ever that simple.

We saw that in the last three chapters, which try to explain how you got your self-image and what you can do to build better self-esteem. Dealing with such a complex, lifelong task reminds me again that it is all too easy to oversimplify any process when you try to capture it in the confines of a few pages in a book. And this is especially true when we turn to our next section, which is modestly titled "How to Win." After many years on the success-seminar circuit, I have come to abhor attempts to put success or winning into a neat set of steps. At the same time, I do believe we need to plan for and take action in specific ways, if we are going to convert theory into reality.

So, we will look at nine areas that I prefer to call skills rather than

"steps to success." Almost anyone can learn these skills. By definition, no-win personalities won't be very interested. These nine
skills are, however, most useful for anyone who wants to win,
whether he prefers the win-lose approach or is trying to switch to
win-win. One subtle difference might be that win-lose people
would tend to put these nine skills into a formula for success.
When your ultimate goal is finishing first or coming out on top of
the heap, formula thinking is often attractive.

Double Winners, I believe, will understand when I call these nine
activities "skill areas." True, the nine skills are in sequence, but
only because life is a sequence that is as inevitable as sunrise-sun-
set.

In what follows, then, I will use the term *winners* as we talk about
how to win. If any obvious differences between the Double Win
and win-lose come up, we'll note them, but for the most part I'll
concentrate on helping anyone who wants to be a winner by putting theory into practice. Winners enjoy and reinforce past successes; they learn from past mistakes; they make decisions in the
present; they set goals just out of sight, but not out of reach, for the
future. The rest of this chapter will talk about the first two skills in
getting on with this process called winning:

1. Decide to take action.
2. Set reachable goals.

In chapter 3, which gave us a profile of the Double Winner, we
discussed the "spectators" who show up to watch the game of life
being played. They are like puppets, caught in the habit of letting
life happen to them. They play their own brand of Trivial Pursuit
by talking about their two favorite subjects: "If only I'da" and
"Someday I'll."

If only I'da finished college. If only I'da not been drafted. If only
I'da married someone rich. If only I'da invested in real estate ten
years ago. If only I'da been good looking. If only I'da got a better
job.

Someday I'll be a Double Winner: when we're out of debt; when
the mortgage is paid off; when the kids are older; when we have a
new president; when my boss retires; when we get a new car; when
I get around to it; when the weather gets better; when I retire.

SKILL AREA ONE:
DECIDE TO TAKE ACTION

Assuming that all of us can stand improvement (and I'll go to the front of the line), a basic decision has to be made to actually do something to change. Action is required.

I appear on Robert Schuller's "Hour of Power" television show every so often and have come to know and admire Dr. Schuller for the "possibilities" he passes on to others. One of his favorite lines that I have pasted on my word processor is: "BEGINNING IS HALF DONE!" I've modified the quote slightly to apply to our subject and now my word processor tells me: "BEGINNING IS HALF WON!" Just by making the decision to get in the arena, I am halfway to victory. (Now if I can just get the "cursor to home," I'll be all set!)

The "If only I'da" and "Someday I'll" excuses keep the spectators sitting in the stands, but never let them play their own game. I know people who live like that. One group is in a town less than two hundred miles from my home in California. The houses there perch less than twenty yards from the San Andreas Fault, with nothing but small backyards between them and a moving canyon. The abyss creeps closer month by month, its progress measurable not in millimeters but in inches at a time.

You would think, as I write, I would be describing a ghost town, once inhabited by families with little leaguers, ballerinas, busy moms and dads, and grandparents. But no, this is an inhabited community whose residents know that the fault will soon swallow their homes through its normal process or possibly engulf them in a sudden earthquake. Yet they remain as they are. They are victims of inertia, lacking the skill or will to change.

The science of physics recognizes two kinds of inertia:

(1) Standing objects tend to remain stationary; (2) moving objects tend to stay in motion.

A simple illustration is to see ourselves as passengers in a car. When the car accelerates from a dead stop, we are in a state of stationary inertia and we tend to remain behind. We feel our mass as we are forced back into the seat. A few miles down the highway, however, a light turns red very suddenly and we slam on our brakes. Our tendency now is to keep right on going, right out of our seats. Only our seat belts prevent us from going through the windshield. We conclude our brief lesson in physics with this rather obvious observation: it's hard to get an object with stationary inertia started and conversely, it is hard to stop an object when it has moving inertia.

The people I worry about most are the ones with "stationary inertia." I constantly come across people who are procrastinating and resisting change. I used to think that their stationary inertia was caused by the fear of failure. But, after years of study and some painful experience of my own, I am convinced that people often procrastinate and resist change because they are afraid of the perceived "costs" of success. And the costs are there:

- taking responsibility to give up bad habits
- setting an example
- distancing yourself from a peer group that isn't helping you succeed
- leading yourself and others down an unfamiliar path
- working more and delaying your own gratification as you work hard to reach a goal
- facing criticism and jealousy

These and other costs of success are why many people escape from the present by occupying their minds with past memories or future expectations. Winners, on the other hand, are not dismayed by the cost of success. They get started and build positive moving inertia. A term most of us may recognize and like better is one we often hear about in sports and in business. Winners get going and build "momentum." They determine to pursue their potential and look forward to an endless dialogue between their talents and the claims of life.

To become a winner, you must assert your option to take responsibility for making the best use of what you have—your mind, your talents, your developed abilities, and that precious commodity called "the time we have to spend on living." You are the only one who can steal your own time, talent, and accomplishments. The choice is yours.

In Skill Area One winning is to make the decision to take action now. And always carry with you the motto "BEGINNING IS HALF WON!"

SKILL AREA TWO:
SET YOUR GOALS

Beginning may be "half won," but there is still a long way to go. The next question is, "Where are we actually headed?" You would be amazed to know how many people fit the following description:

> If you don't know where you're going, you'll end up somewhere else, but it doesn't matter, because you don't recognize where you've been or where you are anyway.

How true that is! The vast majority live by default, not knowing where they want to go, having no need to figure out how to get there. Not specifying their goals, they have no plans to follow, no new habits to develop, no behaviors to rehearse, and no strategies to revise and update. They live by their default settings—those automatic, wired-in putterings that turn minutes into hours and days into months. The mind trips out into tension-relieving, rather than goal-achieving activities.

It is doubtful you would be reading this book if you fit the depressing description above. To develop Skill Area Two in regard to winning, set aside a time and a place for self-examination. Inventory your talents and assets. Then list your liabilities, weaknesses, or other roadblocks you want to remove from your life. What would you like to change? To accomplish? Then set specific goals you are willing to commit yourself to completing. To help you, here are some ideas I often share in my seminars.

The Art of Goal Setting

The more I talk about goals—whether it's with executives in corporate boardrooms or teachers at a convention—the more I realize goal setting is more of an art than an exact science. That's not to say there are not specific things you can do. There are at least seven ways to come at goal setting. What is important is to *do it*. Probably the major reason people are not successful is that they never take the time to define what their goals are and how they plan to reach them.

1. *Make the goals yours.* No goal set for you by others will ever be sought with the same effort and time commitment as one you set for yourself. Ask yourself these questions:

What does winning really mean to me?
What does being successful mean to me?
What do I really want to achieve in my life in the long run?
What are my talents and capabilities?
What am I willing to sacrifice, trade off, or invest in to become more successful?
How will other people benefit from my success?
How will my life be improved by my success?
How will my life be complicated by my success?
Who can I count on to nurture and support me in my pursuits?

Remember, personal goals, the ones you want, are those you will be more likely to achieve. And when you do set personal meaningful goals, keep them to yourself, or share them only with other Double Winners who will take the time to give you positive feedback and input. Remember, misery is always looking for a place to become company. Never share a dream with someone who is likely to rain on your parade.

2. *Set goals with deadlines.* It seems to be an irrevocable part of nature that we work harder toward our goals as our deadlines approach. A goal is not a goal unless it has a deadline. In my seminars, I describe three kinds of temporal goals:

Primary goals—those that can be achieved within the next three to six months.
Intermediate goals—taking from six months to three years. These may include completion of a college degree or vocational training program, reaching middle management in your firm, or the purchase of a new home. Or, they may be stepping-stones in the achievement of . . .
Life goals—taking longer than three years. These include long-term career plans, or those things you'll do in future years, but start preparing for *now*.

And here is another little tip: often it's not enough to put dead-lines on your goals. You need to put "deadlines on your deadlines." Plan out your progress and place time limits on the stages within your goal attainment. For example, "I'll write my next book by May 1" is not enough.

"Section I, comprised of the first two chapters, will be finished by January 15. I'll allot one week to rewriting and proofing; then begin Section II, which should be completed by March 25. . . ." And so on and so on as you shoot for the final goal of manuscript complete by May 1.

3. *Set explicit goals.* Would you ever dream of sending a carrier pi-geon out with the instructions "Deliver this to my cousin Bill"? Would you fire a torpedo with its guidance system instructed to "sink that enemy ship somewhere out there"? Would you ask your son to go to the store with directions to "do the shopping"? Of course not, and your personal instructions to yourself (your goals) should never be vague or general, either. You're after explicit goals—clear and accurate pictures of what you want. The more specific the goal is, the easier it will be to set deadlines for each step along the way. Explicit goals actually give you an inner power that helps you focus your efforts and which drives you forward.

It's ironic—no, tragic—that many people take more time to plan vacations than they do the major parts of their lives. They get deeply involved in selecting a destination, developing a time frame, choosing a method of getting there, figuring costs, trade-offs, and life-style when they arrive. They even get a vinyl, oversized wallet to carry the itinerary (and maybe the traveler's checks).

If a vacation is worth all that trouble, what about becoming better parents or better managers? What does it mean to us? What does it take? What do we need to do more of? When? We need to set aside certain hours and show up at certain times.

On New Year's Eve, instead of going out in search of a hangover, our family congregates around the fireplace to reflect on the events that made the year just past one to remember. We then have our own Oscar presentations at the "Academy Awards Ceremonies for Goals." Each of us opens our sealed envelope, in which we placed our written goals, made on December 31 of the previous year. We then proceed to share our blessings and accomplishments, even though some of us fell short or completely missed the targets we had set twelve months before.

After many years of this type of experience, I can verify that the more defined and specific the goals were, the more often they were reached.

4. *Commit your goals to writing.* Attorneys know the wisdom of the written contract. It demands clarity, specificity, conditions, a time frame, and commitment of money. When all the terms are understood and mutually agreed upon, it usually results in better performance. Incidentally, a good contract is an instrument of a Double Win negotiation.

Before you leave your place of business in the evening, write down at least five personal goals you want to reach the following day. Before you go to sleep that night, prioritize these five personal goals and focus on how you will start reaching them the next morning.

Carry a thirty-day calendar with you at all times and have a twelve-month calendar never more than a briefcase or a purse away from your touch. I carry twelve "legal size" monthly calendar sheets, stapled together, in my briefcase. They can be purchased at any stationery store. On these calendar sheets I write in all my goals, priorities, appointments, projects, and anticipated completion dates. Adapting to changing circumstances and other feedback, I adjust and alter my calendar by correcting each monthly sheet and photocopying the updated sheet so that I have a fresh, accurate (but still flexible) preview of coming attractions.

A support system that I recommend in my seminars consists of three-by-five-inch cards I call "goal minders" or "goal tenders." Each card has a specific self-talk statement, printed or written in the present tense, *as if it has already been achieved.* (For example, "I enjoy fresh fruit for dessert" or "My resting pulse rate is seventy and I'm enjoying increased endurance.") I carry these cards and review them more than once during the day. They help make winning a reflex habit.

5. *Set goals that can be incrementalized and measured.* It's always useful to clarify long-range goals, the ones that have stimulating future benefits that are worth the wait and the work. Long-range goals, however, don't offer you the step-by-step reinforcement and feedback you need for continued motivation. If possible, break your

long-range goals into many short-range ones where you can know the thrill of victory on a smaller scale. Then you can thrive on the many smaller wins, spaced closer together, which will give you a winning pattern that will strengthen you for the long haul toward the bigger long-range goal.

Behavioral psychologists use this method in modifying animal behavior. Remember that circus or county-fair exhibit where the chicken climbed into the fire engine and turned on the siren? Or the ducks that threw tiny sponge basketballs unerringly through the hoops? They were not shown the truck or basketball and expected to learn by trial and error! They were—in psychological terms—"reinforced for successive approximations." Their goals were broken into clearly defined tasks. In a word, they were incrementalized. Here's how it's done:

1. Reward the animal for going near the truck.
2. Once the animal begins spending time near the truck, reward it only if it climbs onto the truck.
3. Once the animal remains on the truck, reinforce it only if it places a leg near the chain that—when pulled—will turn on the siren.
4. Once the leg remains near the chain, reinforce it only when it grabs the chain.
5. Once it holds the chain, reinforce it only when it pulls the chain and starts the siren.

Granted, you and I are not chickens or ducks, but we learn in much the same way. The idea is to set short-term goals that are just beyond your current range of skills. When you miss one of these short-term goals (increments), you review, revise, and retry. When you hit your incremental goal, you reinforce yourself with a positive reward or ceremony. Face the challenge, meet it, or learn from your mistakes, and then move up to the next higher goal.

In a book about physical and mental excellence that I coauthored recently, we used the individual's resting heart rate as an example for setting and reaching incremental goals.[1] Here's how it works:

Your resting pulse may hover in the eighties right now, which is a bit high. You may aspire to bring it into an "excellent condition" range of sixty to seventy, but that's a long-term goal. Your first step is to bring it under eighty, via a combination of aerobics and a nutrition program. When you wake up and find a pulse of seventy-nine after a few weeks, celebrate! Go to a play or concert! Treat yourself to that new hairdo or facial. Rejoice in your successful effort to care for your body and improve your health and longevity. Then set your sights on a resting pulse of seventy-five. Think of all those celebrations on your way to the sixties.

The point is, we all need to win and win again, to develop the winning reflex. Setting step-by-step goals that can be reached, revised, retried, and reinforced works. Wishy-washy daydreaming about pie-in-the-sky payoffs doesn't.

6. *Set goals with pulling power.* When you begin incrementalizing your goals, don't fall victim to setting goals with little or no challenge. Going from a '78 Mustang with four-on-the-floor, to a '79 Pinto with automatic plus power brakes, will hardly stoke the inner fires with motivation. Going from the '78 Mustang to a new Thunderbird is more like it; especially if you have planned, earned, and saved to afford it.

Goals we can reach with little or no effort have no pulling power; they're not the stuff from which winners are made. The excitement of reaching *toward* a challenging goal is often greater than the actual achievement. The joy is more in the reaching than in the grasping. Your goals must be demanding, requiring knowlege, effort, and performance to accomplish. With an honest assessment of your talents and skills, you can set goals that are realistic, believable, and worth working for.

7. *Do your goals pass the Double Win test?* To be true Double Winners in life, we must consider the impact of reaching our goals on other people. Once a goal is defined as to its integrity and merit for our own success, we must ask ourselves a key question before we embark on an action course: "What effect will the realization of my goal have on the others involved?" The answer should be an unequivocal: *beneficial.*

One of the critical aspects of goal setting is that we seldom succeed in isolation, without the support of others. When our own goals match the aspirations of those with whom we come in frequent contact and they, in turn, identify with us, a chain reaction is formed and the whole becomes greater than the sum of its parts. Energy is converted to synergy. The Double Winner is a "goal minder" who becomes a "gold miner" who shares the greater wealth with others.

The Power of Habit

To sum up, we have looked at what we must do to "take our marks" for any race we seek to win. If we prefer living win-lose, we'll want to win mainly for our own glory—our own Gold, if you please. If we seek to live the Double Win, we want others to share in the fruits of victory.

First we saw that we must overcome stationary inertia by deciding to act. Nothing happens until this simple skill (and I do believe it is a skill) is used. But, as valuable as our decisions are, they are worth nothing until we form habits around those decisions to keep ourselves moving.

We have all heard stories, examples, and poems on the power of habit. Here is one in free verse that I especially like:

> You may know me.
> I'm your constant companion.
> I'm your greatest helper, I'm your heaviest burden.
> I will push you onward or drag you down to failure.
> I am at your command.
> Half the tasks you do might as well be turned over to me. I'm able to do them quickly and I'm able to do them the same every time if that's what you want.
> I'm easily managed, all you've got to do is be firm with me.
> Show me exactly how you want it done; after a few lessons I'll do it automatically.
> I am the servant of all great men and women; of course, servant of the failures as well.
> I've made all the great individuals who have ever been great.
> And, I've made all the failures, too.
> But I work with all the precision of a marvelous computer with the intelligence of a human being.
> You may run me for profit or you may run me to ruin, it makes no difference to me.
> Take me. Be easy with me and I will destroy you.
> Be firm with me and I'll put the world at your feet.
> Who am I?
> I'm Habit!

Developing the habit of setting specific goals is invaluable. Until a decision is linked with a definite purpose and specific goals, there is no reason to act on that decision.

It is an unfortunate fact that many motivational rallies, speeches, and books don't result in much change. Many individuals leave these meetings or finish reading self-help books determined to take the action steps that will make them more successful. But soon— sometimes as soon as the next day—they find their determination waning just at the time when they would like to put what they think they have learned into practice. But since a decision is only a promise, the proof is in the purpose, which must be strong enough to convert the decision into a daily habit.

Actually we cannot escape habits. We will deal with our constant companion, Habit, all our lives. Bad habits can destroy our attempts to succeed; good habits can ensure our chances for victory. To make a habit of setting personal reachable goals is a priceless thing, but there are other skills, other habits, to form. Let us see what they are and where they will take us.

LOSERS	WINNERS	DOUBLE WINNERS
Live in the past for the future	Learn from the past, live in the present, and set goals for the future	Learn from the past and work in the present to accomplish goals that benefit everyone's future

8

Get Set
(Are You Prepared?)

A favorite saying of mine is, "You always get out of a garden the fruits of your labor." If you spend time looking at weeds, learning about weeds, hanging around weeds, and planting weeds, you will harvest a big crop of weeds. Saint Paul put it best: "You reap what you sow."[1]

The next four skill areas we will examine all relate to the "you reap what you sow" idea, especially as it pertains to soil preparation. No matter what we're trying to do, we need to prepare. Sometimes these preparations are the long-range variety; others can be done quickly. I have learned that it's important to constantly realize that a certain amount of what I am doing each day is preparing me for some challenge in the future. In finding my own system for preparing, I have discovered four major areas I need to cover to win at anything, whether it's helping my teenage daughter buy a car (which I did just the other day) or conducting a week-long lecture in Australia (from which I just returned).

We looked at Skill Areas One and Two in chapter 7.

The next four skill areas I want to share with you (not "easy steps") are:

3. Get the needed information.
4. Observe winning role models.
5. Simulate (practice) the real thing.
6. Combine relaxation with visualization.

You may be noting that we spent chapter 7 looking at how to get started in a winning effort. Now here in chapter 8 we are still stuck on getting started—that is, preparing for the battle! Out of a total of nine skill areas related to winning, six are being devoted to preparation for the real thing. If this discourages you a bit, remember:

The one-hundred-meter sprint at the Olympics lasts less than ten seconds. How long did the sprinters train for those ten seconds? Other examples from the world of sports are legion. Athletes literally spend years getting ready for a few moments of supreme effort.

The average sales call lasts ten minutes. How much experience and know-how is necessary to close that sale? As I travel around the country speaking to Fortune 500 companies, I find them spending millions of dollars to discover the answer to that very question!

The point is simple. If you want to win, you must be prepared. So, let's get on with it.

SKILL AREA THREE:
GET THE NECESSARY INFORMATION

We've all heard it: "When all else fails, read the instructions!" This old joke remains amusing (sometimes) because it is so basic. We know we should have the facts before we start moving toward a goal, but so often we go in half ready, and wind up with a job half baked—or worse!

As we saw in chapter 7, beginning a battle means you've got it half won. Before starting into battle, however, I have found it helps to have the necessary information to do the job. In behavioral psychologist's jargon it's called "establishing a correct knowledge base."

Be an Open-Minded Skeptic

From where do you get the information you use in your daily efforts to win? I have found that most people rely on their parents, friends, the media, and a variety of individuals with questionable credentials for their knowledge base on how to win. I urge you to spend a few hours this coming week closely examining the sources from which you have gained or are gaining your insights on life. What have been the sources of your "truth"? What are his or her track records and credentials? If challenged, can the information be corroborated?

You will be amazed at how frequently you ingest information from the environment that is no more than speculation, based upon biased opinion. In other cases, you aren't getting information; you're getting titillated by people who are interested in circulation, not education. The *National Enquirer*, for example, advertises itself with a sprightly television ad, complete with bright-eyed, good-looking models who tell you that "people with inquiring minds want to know what the *National Enquirer* has to say." In truth, there is only one good use for scandal sheets like the *National Enquirer*, and I am currently using double-strength-plastic tie bags for the same function.

The fact that the *National Enquirer* claims to have the largest circulation of any newspaper to date should signal to us where the nation is going for its knowledge base. We are a media-oriented society. We live helter-skelter lives, depending on our car radios, TV newscasts, a quick glance at the headlines, and, if we are really on the ball, an hour a week with *Time* or *Fortune*. If, however, you are interested in doing real winning in life, your search for knowledge should take you to libraries, lectures, seminars, and workshops.

Always review credentials from every potential teacher. Within the best of your ability to judge, determine the likelihood that each teacher you choose to hear is prepared with up-to-date, specific information and has a previous record of success in being able to communicate. The world is full of knowledge, but there are only a select few who have the know-how in communicating. Before going to a seminar, for example, try to talk to others who have already attended it. Call or write to these people before you invest time, money—and mind.

Another way to attend seminars and hear speakers at your own convenience is through audio cassettes. Today opportunities to buy or in some cases rent or borrow tape cassettes are just about limitless. You can easily convert your car into a rolling audio learning center. Of the thousands of people I have met in my educational seminars, a large majority credit repeated listening to audio cassettes as the most important resource they have found in making meaningful life changes. Be selective, but be a sponge!

Of course if you are willing to "bite the bullet" and dig out the material for yourself, your greatest untapped resource is that archaic place—little known to all but students trying to finish term papers—"the library."

Early on, while I was in college, my professors taught me to use the library to "check the primary sources." I have lost track of the number of times digging in the library through card-index files, microfiche, and aisles of books helped me turn up facts that had been twisted repeatedly or misquoted by so-called reputable sources.

One interesting, though not terribly significant, example of checking the source revealed for me the fallacy that Albert Einstein failed all his early math and science classes as a young boy. I, like many others, had always made the sweeping generalization in my lectures that Einstein had been something of a dunce while in school and had later climbed out of his intellectual ghetto into greatness. I thought I had read "somewhere" that he had failed his college entrance requirements, but then had gone on to develop the theory of relativity. My audiences always appeared impressed with my encyclopedic reservoir from absolutes. What I was trying to tell them, of course, was, "Anyone can go from dunce to genius." My intentions may have been good, but I was dead wrong about young Albert!

It seems that early in 1984, someone visited a library, got hold of some original sources, and found out that Einstein had not failed his math and science classes at all. What had happened was this: Previous historians had noted that Einstein's top grades of 6, on a grading scale of 1 to 6, had dropped to 1's the following year. Therefore, they assumed Einstein had started flunking all his math and science courses. What actually had happened, however, was that Einstein's high school had reversed its grading system to make the highest grade a 1 instead of a 6!

As my college professors often told me, "Never rely on secondary sources or hearsay evidence." So, I am still learning to view my own knowledge sources as an open-minded skeptic. I'm going to be open-minded enough to listen to a variety of opinions and sources; I want to be skeptical enough to check them out for truth, accuracy, and relevance to my particular needs. Anyone who wants to develop the habit of winning should do the same.

So much for precautions and principles. What is your specific plan or procedure for "establishing a correct knowledge base"? Or, for just "staying informed"?

My personal approach to staying informed is to read our local paper for "need to know" national news and local news that might affect my business or personal life. Also, rather than waste money or time on the "rag" magazines at supermarket checkout counters, I read the national news magazines such as *Time*, *Newsweek*, and *U.S. News & World Report*. (Of the three, I like *U.S. News* for reliability and balance.) Another good source of national news is the newspaper *USA Today*, which is available by subscription or at newsstands.

Because I spend so much time traveling, I have to snatch moments for "increasing my knowledge base" when I can—in airports, during flights, and at "down time" moments in hotels. A key source for me has been *Book Digest*, the little magazine that condenses several of the current leading books in each issue. With a relatively short look at *Book Digest*, I can decide whether or not I want to invest more time in reading the entire volume.

I have already mentioned the vast amount of knowledge available on cassette of seminars, speaker lectures, and sermons. Perhaps you have heard of "Books on Tape," a service that makes current best-sellers and older classics available for rent or purchase.[2] In this way, I can "plug in" to a good book while on a plane or while driving in my car. And it's always fun to ask, "Have you heard a good book lately?"

Two other sources of information are still on the "somewhat exotic" side but will soon be as familiar as the Sunday comics: video cassettes and computer data banks.

Video cassettes are already developing a huge market in the entertainment field, some of which, unfortunately, panders to X ratings and escape fantasy. But there is also a strong market building in video cassettes for "educainment"—how to do things. Courses on gourmet cooking, gardening, and many other subjects are now available on video cassette at college and university extension facilities. Or, if you are fortunate enough to own your own VCR, you can rent or buy video cassettes of your choice.

Those who own personal computers can expand their knowledge by networking with different data banks which put them in touch with a huge national library of information on almost any subject.

The software explosion in computers is nothing short of incredible. You can do just about anything with your computer, from attending college to checking "positions available" in certain fields.

And worth mentioning again is your local library. Make your library card as important as your MasterCard. In our family, we try to have one "reading night" each week. Instead of flipping through the *TV Guide* and gluing ourselves to the tube for the evening, we turn off the TV set and take out our books or other publications that we have decided to read that evening. Sometimes we read individually and sometimes we read together as a family. One thing we have found extremely interesting and valuable is to have someone read out loud from a particularly interesting portion of something he has found. This captures the interest of the entire family and also increases that person's skills in verbal delivery and knowledge of words.

One of the most disturbing things I see is people—including leaders, executives, and managers—depending mostly on television, movies, and a brief glance at the paper for most of their knowledge and inspiration. The knowledge is out there waiting for you. Don't fail to devise your own system, no matter how simple, for building a knowledge base that will help you win in whatever you choose to do.

SKILL AREA FOUR:
SEEK OUT WINNING ROLE MODELS

When the term *role models* is mentioned, many of us automatically think of something needed by children. Parents are supposed to be good role models to kids. So are teachers, coaches, athletes, etc. And, it's true that children do need good role models. The experts have been saying so for a long time. Nearly three hundred years ago René Descartes, French mathematician and philosopher, said: "The chief cause of human errors is to be found in the prejudices picked up in childhood." And George Santayana, the great modern-day philosopher, added this comment, which certainly bears on role modeling: "Children insensibly accept all the suggestions of sense and language. . . ."[3]

But are role models only for children? Santayana also said: "People are not naturally skeptics, wondering if a single one of their beliefs can be reasonably preserved; they are dogmatists, angrily confident of maintaining them all."[4]

The truth is, at any age, we need role models. Not only that, we choose role models whether we realize it or not. That's why, in an earlier chapter, I spent so much time sounding dire warnings about television. Not only is much of television presenting us with limited, biased, and sometimes very warped information; most commercial television is also providing for young and old alike very questionable role models of every size, shape, and philosophy.

In learning how to win, we need to choose role models who not only are winners but who also are worthy of emulation. And we need to just as deliberately reject role models who prove by the conduct of their lives that they are not worth imitating in even the slightest way. One of the greatest career boosts that can happen to you is to find someone who represents what you want very much to become and who also is a fine role model after whom you can pattern your own conduct and attitudes.

The best role model is someone who most nearly approximates who you are, where you've been, and where you want to go. It's not enough to say, "Hey, there's a good role model. He's good looking, trim, wealthy, and confident. Besides, he has alligator-monogrammed shirts. That's who I want to be!"

A good rule is, choose role models you can *learn the most from*, not necessarily ones whom you would *like most to be*. The ones you can learn the most from got where they are by overcoming the same kinds of problems you are facing now. This is the principle that is at work when, for example, successful athletes with roots in the inner-city ghettos return home to motivate the local youth in school and job programs. Having strained and struggled their way out of the streets, they can tell their story to those most needing the motivation. While Tom Watson—the great PGA golfer—could teach anyone a lesson about concentration, hard work, and attitude, he is hardly a perfect role model for inner-city youth. On the other hand, when Earl Campbell or Sugar Ray Leonard speak, the inner-city kids listen.

Who are your role models? Have you chosen at least one or two people in your field whom you want to imitate and learn from? Choosing such role models ties right in with building your knowledge base. If you have favorite authors, teachers, etc., you should have every book they ever wrote and every tape they ever recorded. You should know everything they say backward and forward. There is not much point in having role models unless you are really learning from them.

Of course, you'll discover that Double Winners make the best role models. How can you identify them? That's not hard at all. They will be the ones who will try to help you rather than impress you. They'll not be rushed for time. They'll ask you questions rather than tell you their life stories. And they'll give you specific advice or a lead toward a step forward rather than try to sell you something of their own. You can't miss them. They have *your* interests in mind.

One other thought on role modeling can be found in the "just for fun" quotation you find on a lot of desks and office walls: "How can I expect to soar with eagles when I have to work with turkeys?" The nugget of truth in this little quip is that you become like those with whom you spend your time. Perhaps you cannot always choose the people with whom you work, but you probably have some control over people with whom you spend your spare time. Are they winners—or losers? Are they Double Winners—or win-lose types?

Lord Chesterfield said it well: "We are more than half of what we are by imitation. The great point is to choose good models and to study them with care."[5]

SKILL AREA FIVE:
SIMULATE (PRACTICE) THE REAL THING

When you've made a decision to change, have set reachable goals, and have the right kind of knowledge and role models, the next step is internalization of moves or actions you must use to succeed in reaching your objective. One of the best ways to internalize these actions is simulation.

The word *simulate* means to assume the character of or to imitate. Simulation is a process we have come to closely identify with pilots and astronauts, as a result of watching television coverage of Project Mercury, Project Gemini, Project Apollo, and the Space Shuttle odysseys of our NASA astronauts. Since no one had ever been to the moon prior to Neil Armstrong's touchdown in the Eagle in 1969, scientists at NASA working with broadcast journalists demonstrated moon landings for us in the viewing audience by previewing what it would be like in advance and, subsequently, showing us reenactments of the voyage that were as close to "the real thing" as possible. You recall at the bottom of our television screens during these incredibly true-to-life illustrations the blinking disclaimer: "Simulation only."

Keep in mind, however, that *watching* a simulation on TV is one thing; *doing* it yourself is another. In truth, simulation is not a spectator sport. It is a critical skill to be mastered by those who want to be more proficient in whatever game they want to play. Corporations use simulation in analyzing which product designs will go into actual manufacture. Simulation is used in role-playing drills to ensure production safety on assembly lines. Simulation can play a part in crisis and contingency management exercises. Simulation is often a tool utilized by instructors in sales training programs.

If you would like a vivid example of how one form of simulation works, you might visit a NASA center, a military flight-training "ground school," or an airline-pilot training facility. One such facility, operated by American Airlines in Dallas, Texas, is open for public tours. Here, American Airlines prepares its pilots and keeps them current in instrument flying by using a simulator that is equipped with the same complete cockpit instrumentation that is found in the various types of aircraft flown by American's pilots. Through the use of audio-visual technology in the huge room containing the simulation equipment, the pilots "fly" the simulator through every type of weather condition and foreseeable emergency. They taxi from the ramp, take off, fly to a city, and land, never leaving the ground, of course, but experiencing nearly every sensation that could be encountered on an actual flight.

That's one form of simulation. Another kind can involve actual flying, under carefully rehearsed conditions. I recall one such exercise while in navy flight training. The task to be learned through simulation was low-altitude, high-speed bombing. This was not to be any simulation done in a bolted-to-the-ground Link trainer, which was the kind of equipment we used in those days. This "simulation" took place at twenty thousand feet in real aircraft. Our instructions were to begin a high-speed run at the target, then pull up steady in a 4G climb, lofting our bomb toward the target at the precise moment. We were to continue climbing, go into a loop, and at the top of the loop perform an "Immelmann," a sort of barrel roll, as we escaped the shock blast from the payload. The challenge was to engineer this roll precisely so that the plane was on course back to our aircraft carrier and below enemy radar. This maneuver was not easy, and for our simulation (practice session), we were allowed to do it at twenty thousand feet.

On my first effort, I exited the roll and found myself climbing straight up. My air speed fell to zero, I stalled, and took all of fifteen thousand feet to regain control. On my second try, I overcompensated and exited the roll heading straight down. I started to black out from the excessive "G" force, felt the wings shudder under the strain, and again used about fifteen thousand feet to recover. For someone who was supposed to be able to accomplish this maneuver over and over without incident, I was definitely not doing too well.

We regrouped in the debriefing room, where most of us were commended for a training session well done. As a group, we had done so well that tomorrow we were going to do it for real! Our high-speed run would be at fifty feet above the desert floor! From the back of the group, I managed to squeak out a question: "Sir, at the highest point of our pull-up, how high will we be?" Our commanding officer answered, "At the highest point, you should be no more than nine hundred feet above the terrain."

I then told him that I probably wouldn't have enough room and explained that in my two practice runs at high altitude, I had taken fifteen thousand feet to come out of it and that if I tried it tomorrow, I'd probably dig a hole 14,100 feet deep in the desert floor!

"Could I please make a few more high-altitude simulation runs tomorrow, and then join the rest of the team later?" I asked with a dry throat.

"Lieutenant Waitley," he said, "you can go back and do it at twenty thousand feet until you get it right. But remember, you may not always have the extra day or second chance in the real world. That's why it's so important to practice correctly in the simulation drills. Your life and the lives of your buddies may depend on it!"

The next day, I did my simulations correctly and managed to stay within the nine hundred-foot limit. Later, I flew the real thing with confidence. But I never forgot that lesson. Simulation is an invaluable skill to help prepare you for all kinds of situations. Some of them could be called "life and death": flying a plane, driving a car, using a parachute, or even teaching children the procedures in crossing busy intersections, and how to respond to fire alarms at school. But simulation can also play a vital role in developing selling and negotiating skills, in product design and manufacture, in high-performance athletic competition, in the arts, in learning how to parent, and in public speaking.

In a word, practice under realistic conditions can make perfect.

Using Simulation to Learn How to Speak

For example, in public speaking, the process of simulation could be developed in the following manner:

Suppose you have always wanted to speak in public about the Double Win, because you believe it is so important. You have made the decision to go ahead and do it, rather than tell your friends that "someday" you'd like to start. You have researched the library for examples of Double Win case histories and principles. You have attended lectures and observed both the content and delivery manner of the speaker. You have listened to cassettes of speakers who approximate your own age, background, and beliefs. You have written a twenty-minute speech and have rehearsed it in the privacy of your bedroom until you have it memorized, but the rehearsal in your bedroom *is not* really simulation.

To simulate, you must present it to real people in a setting as near to the actual situation as possible. I started with my family. They listened patiently and offered feedback and suggestions. (One member suggested I consider a different avocation.) During this family simulation exercise, I rehearsed in front of a nurturing support group who would be honest but constructive in their feedback.

From the family simulation, I moved out into more challenging waters. I drilled my public-speaking skills in front of friends whom I invited to dinner. They got my after-dinner speech for dessert. Here again, the setting was casual, supportive, and nonthreatening. If you'll pardon the pun, it was a piece of cake!

After several speeches to my friends, I proceeded to conditions that were as close to the real thing as possible. I contacted Rotary, Kiwanis, Optimists, and women's service clubs who meet weekly or monthly for lunch or dinner. There was no fee or honorarium paid to me. These groups were accustomed to a variety of guest speakers, from high-school essay-contest winners to local politicians, talking on every imaginable subject.

Today, I deliver about two hundred keynote addresses each year to major corporations, institutions, and public audiences on the Psychology of Winning and the Double Win. When I am asked how long it took me to earn the fees I am receiving today, I answer politely that I delivered over eight hundred unpaid "keynote simulations" before I was ever paid a cent for doing a real one.

The keys to simulation are:

Learn technique from a positive role model.
Memorize the material in exact sequence of performance.
Rehearse the performance until mastered.
Drill in realistic but nonthreatening environments until the successful performance becomes second nature.
Ask for critique from your role model, teacher, coach, or supportive family or friends and get their feedback before you go out into the "world class" arena.

Other Ways to Use Simulation

Simulation can be used in almost any activity:

Sales representatives simulate by going through their presentations in front of peers who offer them as many realistic objections to their product or service as possible to give them experience in confronting what it could be like during a "real" sales call.

Seminar leaders, teachers, and other performers who have to present material to groups can simulate their programs with dress rehearsals. If possible, have an audience who can give you feedback.

Hostesses can even simulate in preparation for an important dinner party or other social function. They can walk through each step, from helping people park, greeting the guests at the door, taking their coats, seating them at the table, serving the refreshments, adjourning to the living room, and going through the entertainment or social part of the evening in complete detail. You may not feel it is necessary to go over every function minutely, but you will be amazed at the value of doing a "dry run" on the entire event. All kinds of gremlins and glitches can appear and you can correct them before the real guests arrive.

The beauty of the simulation skill is that it allows you to perform and "get it right" without the fear of failure creating stifling or choking pressure. When you face actual high-performance action (the real thing), it will be almost like another simulation drill. With simulation, you can raise your self-image thermostat into a new "comfort zone." Setting new sights and reaching for new heights is no longer an uncomfortable prospect; it's an exciting, stimulating challenge.

SKILL AREA SIX:
RELAXATION AND VISUALIZATION

The final skill area in the preparation part of winning is the merging of visualization and relaxation techniques to assist you in the practice, concentration, and correction phases of goal achievement. When you relax, both physically and mentally, your ability to learn, remember, and perform is enhanced. In sports, for example, relaxation plays an important role in allowing athletes to recall more vividly the correct execution or delivery of difficult maneuvers. The relaxation process also helps reduce the tightening up (choking) tendencies associated with precision performance, thereby reducing costly mistakes and preventing injuries.

Relaxation is normally thought of in terms of relief of the distresses of life and coping with frustration and anxiety, leaving us more energy for positive pursuits and reducing potential health problems. More recently, relaxation through guided imagery has been used to place the mind and body in the most receptive states for training and for actual performance in athletic, corporate, professional, artistic, and personal areas of our lives.

Take a Trip in Your Mind

I have become a great believer in the visualization/relaxation combination. The winners I know have a calm assurance about them because they are well prepared. They visualize the act of winning before it ever happens. Not only do they practice and simulate relentlessly but they also act like winners outside of the arena or office, imagining with words, pictures, and feelings the roles they want to play.

There is a direct relationship between visualization and actual performance. Edmund Jacobson, an American physiologist, has conducted studies which show that when a person imagines running, small but measurable amounts of contraction take place in the muscles associated with running.[6] The same pathways in the brain are stimulated by imagined running as by actual running, and this holds true with any other physical or mental activity.

When a person holds a vivid, fearful picture in his or her imagination, the body responds, through the autonomic nervous system, with a feeling of uneasiness, upset stomach, elevated pulse and blood pressure, sweating, and dryness of the mouth. Conversely, when an individual holds a pleasant, relaxing image in his or her mind, the body responds with a lowered heart rate, decreased blood pressure, and relaxed muscles. What the mind harbors, the body manifests.

Valeri Borzov, the great Russian sprinter who won two gold medals in the sprints in Munich in 1972, described his mental state in an interview after the meet:

> "As I placed my feet against the starting blocks, I began to run the race in my mind. The spectators, naturally, could not know this. They only saw Borzov walk slowly to the starting line, carefully place his feet against the starting blocks, and freeze in that pose until the command 'Ready!' Mentally, though, I was somewhat ahead of that. I was already running. By learning to draw a mental picture of the race while I was still at the starting line, I was able to react to the starting shot with split-second speed. And when the shot was fired, my inner robot—programmed to get me out of the motionless state—switched on and took over."[7]

Bobby Fischer, the great chess master, worked many moves ahead before making a physical move of a playing piece. Not only did he visualize his own playing moves but he also played out in his mind nearly every likely response by his opponent.

And who can ever forget the TV close-ups of Dwight Stones,

supposedly over the hill in his thirties, talking to himself, rocking his head and arms in motion with imagined strides, and the explosive lift-off of his left leg, just before making the American high jump record at the Olympic trials in Los Angeles in 1984. Stones proved the experts, who said he was too old and had lost the competitive edge, wrong through superb physical conditioning and mental preparation.

To enhance your ability to relax and visualize, start taking mental notes of all the worthwhile sensual experiences in your life. Take in as many sights, sounds, smells, textures, and tastes as you can. Feel the texture of wet sand or cool grass between your toes. Smell the sea air at the ocean or smell the newly mowed hay as you drive through the country. Notice the colors. Be more curious and aware about everything in the environment.

As you listen to someone talk, try to form a mental image of the situation he or she describes. Allow the words to form images, feelings, and sensations. When you converse with others, use words that are rich in visual imagery. You will enjoy a side benefit of becoming a better conversationalist and public speaker if you do.

For your general-visualization exercise, pick an imaginary or special place to visit in your mind during a ten- to fifteen-minute period when you can relax without interruption. You may want to recall a pleasant time and place in your life; for example, a vacation. Close your eyes and let your attention drift back to that scene. Remember the feelings you had at the time and relive them as you allow the images to come into your mind. By linking feelings and images, you will be able to recall both better. Focus on one especially memorable part of one of the experiences: how it looked, what you heard, how you felt, and what you did. Recreate the episode in your imagination as vividly as possible.

As with any skill, you'll improve with practice. Returning to the same place will let you speed the learning process, but you can take yourself to any destination you desire. You may experiment with soft, slow, relaxing music in the background, and vary the positions you relax in to find the most comfortable. You are in control; this isn't a magical hypnosis technique. It's you and your creative inner self taking a brief journey. Following are some suggestions for taking a trip in your mind. Try it—you'll like it!

An Exercise in Visualization

Place yourself in a comfortable position and try these "spot visualizations." Quick enough to slide into your few idle moments during the day, they'll further develop your skills and make winning that much easier. Using your inner senses of sight, touch, smell, sound, and taste, visualize the following:

> The sight of an old barn in the country . . .
> The way your living room looks . . .
> The face of your mother or father . . .
> Fourth and one on the one-yard line . . .
> The touch of a loved one . . .
> The feel of velvet . . .
> > of warm sunshine on your face . . .
> > of nubby corduroy . . .
> The smell of fresh-cut oranges . . .
> > of a barbecue grill loaded with burgers . . .
> > of your favorite perfume or men's cologne . . .
> The sound of the ocean . . .
> > of a jet plane . . .
> > of a twelve-cylinder Ferrari . . .
> The taste of fresh apple pie . . .
> > of a sour pickle . . .
> > of broiled lobster . . .

Relax, enjoy the feeling, then return slowly. Practicing these exercises over and over will help you use visualization and relaxation as a practical tool in your professional life, in your pursuit of better health and longevity, and in your personal relationships as well.

As you gain skill in relaxation, you will find yourself opening up and being willing to make more honest assessments of what you are doing, where you are going in your life, and who you are becoming. If possible, this weekend take a long walk in the woods, by a lake, or up a mountain trail. Take a long bike ride, or jog on the beach. As you observe the wonder and abundance of nature, review the six skill areas we've covered in the last two chapters. Where have you been selling yourself short? Where have you failed to develop the potential you know is there?

Go back over these six skill areas. Remember that making decisions to actually do something is a skill that you need to develop and use continually. And then, are you setting the right goals? Are they big enough to stretch you but not so far out of reach that they are a detriment instead of a help? What about your sources of information and knowledge? If you're depending on newspapers and the networks for most of what you "know," you are selling yourself short. A veritable gold mine of books and tapes is out there waiting for you. Never stop seeking out more qualified and appropriate role models who give you Double Win vibrations. Do all the simulating you can. Practice, not wishful thinking, makes perfect. And then use relaxed visualization to forecast successful performances.

All right, you've taken your mark, and you're set. Now it's time to get out there and go for the Double Win!

LOSERS	WINNERS	DOUBLE WINNERS
Make promises they never keep	Make commitments to themselves and keep them	Make commitments to themselves and to others and keep both

9

Go!
(Are You Concentrating on Winning, or on Something Else?)

Your preparation for winning is complete. You've made the decision . . . set incremental goals . . . developed the knowledge base . . . found appropriate role models . . . learned to simulate, relax, and visualize.

Now comes the real test. *You've got to go out and actually do it.* The key to success in performance is the ability to take your preparation and concentrate your action on the *desired result,* without considering (during performance) the *penalties of failure* and the things that can go wrong.

That's why skills like simulating, relaxing, and visualizing are so important. Those dry runs are the times you can afford to fail. You can correct your errors as many times as necessary until you have your Immelmann loop right. When it's time for the "real thing," ideally you won't worry about taking a plunge. You will already have been through all that before, when you practiced so diligently with simulation.

Theoretically, all you will have to do is "do it." But of course, we all know it is not that easy. Let's break the process down into the last three skill areas and see how it works.

7. Concentrate and do it.
8. Monitor your performance with feedback
9. Reset your goals and try again.

Naturally, these three skill areas are the most interesting and fun. Here's where the action is! But one more word about the first six skills covered in the last two chapters. Without decisions made, goals set, knowledge learned, role models observed, followed by simulating, relaxing, and visualizing, your performance record will range from fair to poor. I see it happen all the time with executives, managers, coaches, parents—anyone. You can roar into action without proper background and preparation and fall flat on your face, often bringing others down with you. The Boy Scouts are right: "Be prepared!" To not prepare invites despair!

SKILL AREA SEVEN:
CONCENTRATE AND DO IT

Sounds straightforward enough, so why is it so hard? Perhaps the greatest lesson to learn about concentrated action is to focus all your attention on the desired result and dismiss the background noise and potential penalties of failure.

"Just concentrate and you'll sink that free throw. What if the score is tied, the clock has run out, the crowd is going insane, and you missed your last two? Just concentrate!"

"Type this letter for me, and try not to make any mistakes. I need it in five minutes for the board meeting. Just concentrate!"

"Concentrate, Webster. These sales are critical. The survival of our division depends upon your output."

"Your grades are terrible. Blow this final and no car for a month!"

"I expect more performance out of this production department. Layoffs will continue unless we can turn things around."

Perhaps the second greatest lesson to learn about concentration is: "Don't tell yourself what not to do." The brain is a fascinating machine. Program it with a negative idea and it's extremely difficult to focus on the positive. For example:

"Remember, don't pitch to this guy low and inside, he loves it."

So, you try to throw it up and away and . . . good-bye ball game.

"Now remember, don't call Barbara by her nickname. She hates Barbie." So, you are introduced and, "I've really looked forward to meeting you, Barbie. . . ."

Once the brain is locked in on what you *don't* want, it's almost impossible to get away from it. I once had opportunity to play in a foursome with Lee Trevino during the Andy Williams San Diego Open, which I originated as a charity benefit for the Salk Institute. Just before our group teed off in the Pro-Am, Lee did a little psych job on us: "Do you fellas breathe in or out during your back-swing?"

I tried not to think about it as I whipped my drive back in front of three thousand Trevino groupies. We never did find my ball!

Now Children, Don't Touch the 240Z!

I'll throw in a third lesson I've learned about concentrated action: Don't give negative instructions to others, especially your children. In other words, *don't tell them what you don't want them to do.*

When one of my daughters turned sixteen and I had just bought a new Datsun 240Z, after considerable stretching of the budget, we made a deal. I was to drive the Z at first and she would get to drive it after adequate practice sessions with me riding shotgun.

I was leaving town on a business trip and our first driving lesson in the new Z was to take place on my return. My daughter, along with her brothers and sisters, were lined up and I gave them all the word on what was *not* to occur in my absence. I paced up and down in front of them like Rommel before a panzer sortie into North Africa during World War II.

"I'll be out of town for two days and two nights," I said, eyeing each of them. (They had a habit of not tattling on one another, so I always had to assemble them for group briefings, like the Von Trapp family.)

"These are the keys to my new, burnt-orange racy 240Z. I am putting them here on my dresser, and I don't want any of you to touch them, especially the older young lady here with the smile on her face.

"Upon my return," I continued, "she will learn to operate this powerful driving machine in a manner so as to assure the safety of the vehicle, the passengers, and the passersby." (I was really beginning to sound like Rommel!)

"Are there any questions about what I don't want to happen while I'm gone?" I interrogated. They shook their heads in unison. "Good," I said, "whatever you do, don't anyone take those keys on top of the dresser and drive my new car." They went back to play and later that night, after saying good-byes, I took the red-eye to Washington, D.C.

I was having a late dinner meeting the next evening when the call came in. The conspiracy had unfolded quickly. The keys had vanished from my dresser and reappeared in the ignition of the 240Z. My daughter had driven the car about two miles to downtown La Jolla and had parked it—with engine still running—in front of Walker Scott's Department Store. Her high-school friends were painting Halloween scenes on all of the merchants' storefront windows as part of an annual celebration at which prizes were awarded for the most creative renderings.

When her friends asked her how the engine sounded, she revved the motor. Somehow, in a manner known only to beginning teenage drivers, the gear train got engaged and she drove the 240Z into the department store, through Jewelry, Lingerie, and Kitchenware, finally coming to a halt in Sofabeds. The car was totaled, but miraculously neither my daughter nor any of the store patrons were injured.

At least her timing had been perfect. When she hit the front door and made her grand entrance into Walker Scott's Department Store, it was 5:01, one minute after the last customer had left and the store had closed. Apparently only the glass doors, several aisles of consumer goods, the car, and my daughter's dreams had been shattered. She was physically unharmed, but visibly shaken up and taken to the hospital for observation.

I arrived as quickly as possible and found her suffering mostly from remorse.

"Dad, I'm so sorry and so ashamed. I'll bet you're just furious, aren't you?" she whispered.

I held her hand and reassured her, "On the contrary, sweetheart, I'm relieved and grateful that no one was hurt and that you are all right."

She fought back her tears and asked, "What did I learn from this, Dad?"

"How to make monthly payments," I offered. "You have to pay for the damage to the store, and help me pay for the car. But don't worry, in about three years it will be taken care of and then we can think about another car for you. Besides, look at the experience you will have in financial management!"

When she recovered from the shock, she asked me another question: "What did you learn from this experience, Dad?"

I thought for a moment and then answered, "I learned to take my car keys with me and to tell my kids what I expect of them, *not* what I *don't* expect of them."

This daughter of ours (we have four) has matured into a beautiful young woman. She is a hard worker, talented, service-oriented, and incidentally, a good driver with an excellent record. We laugh about this story together, and she knows that I tell it to teach others constructive behavior, not to embarrass her.

Focus on the Immediate Task

"Each problem carries a past and a future. . . . If you concentrate on the present, you eliminate two thirds of the problem!"

These are the words of Dr. Sidney Rosen, who wrote a book with the late Milton Erickson, the renowned hypnotherapist, entitled *My Voice Will Go With You: The Teaching Tales of Milton H. Erickson, M.D.* Erickson liked to use golf to illustrate his ideas for taking positive steps to avoid negative thinking. For example, he would advise a golfer to play every hole as if it were the first hole. The point was, you didn't have to worry about doing as well on the third hole as you did on the first. Because each hole was the "first" hole, you could take your best shot.

In commenting on Erickson's theory, his coauthor, Dr. Rosen, observes that Erickson realized if you concentrate on the present, you eliminate two-thirds of the problem. By playing each hole as if it were the first, "You have eliminated the past, and . . . the future can only be one of positive expectancy."[1]

In other words, don't remember what went wrong, simply look ahead to making things go right. A loser thinks, *There's the sand trap.*

I remember what happened in last week's round. Better play it safe. (Sure enough, he plays it safe, right into the middle of the trap!)

One of the best methods for concentrating is to step back just before the performance, use your relaxation/visualization skills, and picture exactly what you want to accomplish as if you were doing it perfectly. I see this time and time again on the PGA golf tour. I also have studied the concentration of Raphael Septien, the great place kicker on the Dallas Cowboys football team and leading scorer in the NFL. As he swings his leg and his toe meets the ball, his dominant thought at the moment of impact is, *Follow through and the ball is up and between the goalposts.*

The secret of concentration is to stop stewing, relax, and start doing. Always talk yourself toward the goals and the rewards of success, not away from what you don't want. Forget failures from the past. Focus on the present task at hand and make winning your dominant thought.

SKILL AREA EIGHT:
MONITOR YOUR PERFORMANCE WITH FEEDBACK

The way in which you supervise your performance, feeding back to yourself whether you're winning or losing, is a critical but often neglected step in goal achievement. Winning once or twice is relatively easy. It's *staying on top* that's tough, because people go back to being "themselves." What you need to develop is what I call the "positive feedback process." If you can learn to give yourself the right feedback, you will turn goal achievement into a habit.

During the feedback process, you analyze (play back) your performance, always being sure to carefully massage your self-image and reinforce yourself with positive self-talk. For example, winning efforts should be greeted with positive statements like, "I can be proud of that lecture," or "I earned my highest commission ever last month," or "My daughter knew she could trust me and I'm glad she told me her problem."

You can also use the feedback process if things haven't gone so well. Efforts that come up short can be met with, "I can do better than that," or "That's not like me. I'll prepare more and get it right the next time."

Following are some examples of the loser's use of the feedback process. I am including examples of poor feedback when you're failing and poor feedback when you're succeeding. (I also suggest what could have been good feedback in each situation.)

A basketball player goes out to practice free throws. His coach is upset because his free-throw percentage is down to 58 percent and he has cost the team several games lately because of too many missed shots.

He fires up three or four free throws and they all bounce off the rim, just short. He's failing—again—and doesn't help himself any when he mutters: "I just can't make free throws. I'll just have to hope they don't foul me as often."

(Winning feedback here could be something like this: "A little more arch, follow through—you can do it!")

Or, suppose our basketball player starts shooting some practice shots and drops five or six in a row. He can give himself losing feedback here also, and it would sound like this: "Wow, what's happening? This isn't like me. This can't last."

And it doesn't—he goes right back to missing three out of five or more.

(Winning feedback in this situation would have sounded like this: "That's it. You can make free throws as well as your jumper. Let's keep it going!")

Or, take the weekend duffer who uses up just about every ball in his bag on the first three holes because they border a lake, a freeway, and somebody's backyard. His losing feedback in the face of this kind of failure might sound like this: "I never could drive. My slice is incurable."

(Winning feedback here could be this: "You need more pull from your left hand—and get your hips around. You can hit it straight—let's do it right!")

Or, suppose our duffer drives the first three holes like he's Jack Nicklaus. Can he use poor feedback in the face of such wonderful success? Of course he can. On the fourth tee he mutters to himself, "This can't last. I'm playing out of sight." And his next drive does just that—out of sight into the woods.

I actually had this happen to me in a round of golf I played with friends a few years ago. I had played the front nine in a style that would have made my high-school friend Gene Littler proud. As we approached the tenth tee, the guy keeping the scorecard said,

"What's gotten into you, Waitley? You shot thirty-six on the front nine—perfect par!"

"I did?" I gulped. "How can that be? I'm not a par golfer!"

Sure enough, on the back nine, I went right back to the old "Waitley's Eighties," shooting a forty-four.

(And what would correct feedback have sounded like in that situation? Well, I could have said: "Wow! Perfect par! Now you're getting it. Keep swinging through the ball. You always did know you could break eighty. Today's the day you're going to do it!")

Or, let's consider the shy young man who wants to ask out a pretty woman he's had his eye on for some time. He builds up his courage, dials her number, and tries to keep his voice from squeaking as he pops the question. The goddess politely declines. Giving himself bad feedback he mourns: "I knew I should have had my teeth straightened. What made me think she would go out with me?"

(Correct feedback might have said: "She probably already had plans. Or maybe she doesn't feel she knows me well enough. I'll wait and try again in a few weeks.")

Or, suppose our potential suitor is in luck, and the lady accepts his invitation. Can he give himself bad feedback now? Of course he can: "She probably won't have a good time, and I'll never see her again." He takes her to dinner, dunks his tie in his soup (or worse, in *her* soup), and blushes uncontrollably every time he tries to converse.

(And what would good feedback have been? "We're going to have such a great time! I know this date has been worth waiting for.")

Gary Player, one of golf's immortals, gave an impromptu lesson on how to correct performance through positive feedback during the Masters Tournament several years ago. He lined up his shot, deftly swung his seven iron, and laid the ball down softly, but thirty feet past the pin. Now, I realize that for most of us, to put the ball thirty feet from the pin would be sensational. But for Player, that was a little too far to putt for a birdie. He wanted to "correct his error."

Without a shift of expression, he looked at his caddie, who handed him his eight iron. He walked back to where the ball had been. He went into his stance, gave the club head its usual waggle. He paused, glanced at the target, then swung and watched the imaginary ball land dead to the pin.

You could almost see him saying to himself, *That's the way to play it. That's better. Next time I'll put it right in there.*

You and I should use the same principle in any activity or situation during daily life. When our children do something wrong we should say, "That is not like you," or "You're more capable than that behavior shows," or "You'll do it better next time." A good principle to follow is "Always feed back to the target." The better coaches don't just criticize, they use game films to help the team correct to the target—to figure out what's wrong and how to change it. This kind of feedback helps the players change their goals where necessary, but it's always headed in a positive direction.

The thing to remember is don't just criticize what you've done. Instead, realize you've simply missed the target because of incorrect information. Send yourself a message called, "Target correction necessary." A failure is only a growth experience that requires new data, more practice, and a new effort of concentration that says, "This time I'll do it right."

What Kind of Feedback Is Best?

It won't surprise you to learn that the best place to turn for feedback is inside. In Part II we looked at just how our self-image works. We learned about resetting our self-image thermostat on win-win. Your self-image thermostat is a critical instrument in engaging in a proper-feedback process. Following are some questions you can use as you go about trying to reach goals you have set:

Do I feel good about my progress today? This week? This month? This year?

Am I going where I carefully decided I want to go? If not, have my feelings about the destination changed, or have I veered from the plotted course?

Am I becoming the person, the Double Winner, that I hope to be? How do people respond to me? Do they seem to be saying, "Yes, I like myself best when I'm with you"? Or, does their nonverbal communication seem to say, "I don't like your one-way-win attitude"?

Am I practicing the Double Win, or imagining it? Do others want to talk with me, come to me for advice, be like me? If not, what can I change?

Is my body signaling distress? Are my goals the kind that give me just enough motivation to stretch myself, or am I being too ambitious? Am I feeling irritable and frustrated? Do I communicate this to others? Am I having trouble sleeping? Am I eating unusually more or unusually less? Are my energy levels down to "low"? Am I puttering around, majoring in minors, watching TV shows the real winner in me would never bother with?

How does what I'm doing now compare with my last best effort? Have I made the necessary efforts and taken the right steps to get back on target toward my goal? Are my goals really mine? If so, are they realistic in terms of what I've done so far and what I can do in the future?

Note one thing about the above questions. Many of them involve goals. If your goals aren't personal and explicit, you'll have no chance in reaching them with *any* kind of feedback. The answers to these critical, internally directed questions can help you reach your goal only if that goal is truly yours and one you know you can accomplish.

Feedback From Others Can Be Helpful If . . .

Since the all-knowing, all-seeing and all-feeling Double Winner has yet to be born, there are many times when feedback from those around us can be helpful. Your efforts to reshape your self-image and build high self-esteem won't "build Rome in a day." While you're busy restructuring your internal environment, those people in your external world can be priceless in supplying goal-targeted feedback. Or they can be deadly. I'd be embarrassed to state a rule this obvious if I hadn't already seen it broken a thousand times:

Get feedback only from those people
who are truly interested in seeing you reach your goals.

Misery loves company. Surpass the achievements of your social crowd or your business colleagues and look out for the slings and arrows of the many who wish you were back where they are. In a word, it's called jealousy. Always try to pay the most attention to those who love you, want the best for you, and will help you because you helped them when *they needed it.*

But beware, motives and fears run deep. A win-lose boss who supports and comforts you when you're down may like you best when you are in just that state. Start succeeding and challenging his insecurities and don't expect his feedback to be objective and well-intentioned.

Even parents aren't immune to emotional conflicts that can taint their feedback. Many a parent has had difficulty accepting the success of a child, and without a conscious or evil thought, has still fed back "Oh, *you* can't do that" information.

Spouses often outgrow each other. A husband left behind by a wife who has "gotten out of the house" and mixed career with homemaking, can feel so much envy and anger that it eliminates him from being a helpful feedback source.

At best, even with those who love us and would die for us, getting correct feedback is difficult. That's why you should always rely on internal feedback more than anything else. When you know yourself, there's no question of trust and motives. The best source of feedback for you is *you.*

SKILL AREA NINE:
RESET YOUR GOALS AND TRY AGAIN

Perhaps the most important dominant thought in the feedback process is, "Failure is just a learning experience. No problem, try again."

I've always liked the true story of a clergyman, then in his fifties, who gave up and quit without reaching one of his major goals. He had written a manuscript and sent it to a host of publishers without success. With his stack of rejection notices piled high, he threw the manuscript in the wastebasket in frustration. As his wife reached in to salvage it, he told her sternly, "We've wasted enough time on it. I forbid you to take it from the wastebasket."

The following day she made a decision to try another publisher. When she arrived, the publisher noticed that her parcel looked odd, unlike any book he'd ever seen. It was too big, bulky, and the wrong shape to be a manuscript. When he unwrapped the clumsy package wrapped in brown paper, the publisher discovered a wastebasket containing a manuscript that we have come to know as *The Power of Positive Thinking* by Dr. Norman Vincent Peale. Had his wife, Ruth, not dared to reset his goal and try again, we probably would never have seen Dr. Peale's book, which has sold more than 30 million copies to date.

Persistence means giving full concentration and effort to whatever you're doing right now. It means being happy with your work, but hungry for more knowledge, feedback, and progress. It means making more calls, going more miles, getting an earlier start in your day, and always being on the lookout for a better way of doing what you're doing. Persistence is success through trial, error, resetting your goals, and moving toward the target.

Whenever you make a change in your life-style or performance, anticipate a temporary drop in productivity and efficiency. Don't worry if the change isn't bearing fruit right away. As familiarity and confidence rebuild, the productivity will increase again.

If you fail the first time, try again immediately. If you fail again, check your feedback and reset your goal, then try a second time. If you fail again, your sights may be too high for now, or you may need more knowledge or practice.

Oh, yes, one more thing: *Never give up!*

LOSERS	WINNERS	DOUBLE WINNERS
React negatively	Respond effectively	Reinforce successfully

PART IV

Living the Double Win

We have looked at the difference between win-lose and win-win.

We have examined the summum bonum of the Double Win: self-esteem.

We have considered nine critical skill areas to learn how to build our own approach to "how to win."

And now it's time to think specifically about living by the shepherd's staff of the Double Win, not the sword of win-lose. We have already seen that you can live the Double Win anywhere—at work, at home, at school, and on the athletic field. Perhaps, however, we need one more look at the two areas that touch almost all of us—our jobs and our families.

Will the Double Win work in the corporate jungle? Come and see.

Can the Double Win work at home, where rhetoric and idealism can melt faster than butter in a jet afterburner? If the Double Win is for real, we'll find out behind closed doors—in our homes with our families.

Finally, we'll take a look at our society as it gropes its way toward the end of the twentieth century. What are our chances for moving beyond survival to growth and fulfillment? Can the Double Win help? Some would say maybe. Others—myself included—believe it's our only chance.

10

Can the Double Win Work in the Workplace?

It's a fair question that might be asked by cynic or skeptic. The Double Win sounds like a nice idea for "civilized" settings where people can afford to say, "If I help you win, then I win, too." But can it really work on any widespread basis in the corporate jungle, where the bloody law of tooth and claw reads:

Our goal is maximum return for the stockholders.

And why shouldn't that be the law in a corporation? The shareholders are, after all, the owners of the business who are putting their money at risk, usually with no assurance of return and relying on the company's management to make it fly. If there is such a thing as a "corporate conscience," what should a corporation be conscientious about?

What indeed? Some would say corporations have no conscience as far as their employees are concerned. It's a win-lose war out there and the company troops are used up much like soldiers. If anyone burns out, he can be replaced by reinforcements straight out of Harvard, or other business-school boot camps.

The horror stories are familiar and well documented: long hours, stuffed briefcases, dinners with clients while wives and children wait, and wait some more.

There is also the feared phenomenon some call the "IBM syn-

drome." It is ironic that giant IBM, which is so respected for its
management and passionate desire to serve its customers, and does
so much for its personnel in other ways, is also wryly described by
its own employees like this: "I work for IBM, which means '*I've
Been Moved!*' " How *does* a junior executive sell his wife on any
Double Win advantages in uprooting the children and moving two
or three thousand miles to the new branch office where opportunity
supposedly beckons?

And how does the Double Win fit into those companies in the
fast lane of padded expense accounts, price fixing, and bribes?
Then, too, there is the frequent bloodcurdling tale of the faithful
employee who spends thirty years doing a good, if not always brilliant, job for the firm, only to be found obsolete or unneeded with
just a few years left before becoming fully vested in the retirement
program.

I know all these problems are there. I speak in hundreds of corporation settings annually, and I am well aware that I've only
touched on a few of the more obvious pitfalls awaiting any starry-
eyed idealists bold enough to practice the Double Win in the
marketplace.

Nevertheless, I am optimistic and get more so every day. I believe
in free enterprise and fair competition in the marketplace. And I
believe in corporations, which provide thousands of jobs and most
of our Gross National Product. Instead of criticizing them, I prefer
to help them spot their flaws and do something to improve. (Could
there be a Double Win in there someplace?)

Without question, the Double Win is not the prevailing philosophy practiced by most corporations today. But then, the Double
Win is not the prevailing philosophy practiced anywhere today. As
we have admitted several times, win-lose rules the roost, but I believe win-lose is hearing footsteps (which ought to make that particular mentality *very* nervous!).

I've already alluded to several companies where, if the Double
Win is not in full bloom, it is at least poking its stubborn head up
through cracks in the parking-lot asphalt. We've already looked at
several firms where Double Win concepts are in clear evidence:
Tandem Computer, General Electric, Ko-Rec-Type, Frito-Lay, and
Tupperware. Dozens more can join the list. Just a few of the many
best-run companies which provide lessons taught by *In Search of*

Excellence include: Data General, Texas Instruments, Hewlett-Packard, Wang, Maytag, Procter & Gamble, Avon, Johnson & Johnson, Levi Strauss, Marriott, McDonald's, Delta, Citibank, Caterpillar, Deere, Minnesota Mining and Manufacturing, Boeing, and Du-Pont.[1]

But, no matter what the company, we must note a key point. On any corporate stage where the Double Win is being enacted on any scale, large or small, you will find a person (or persons) with a self-image thermostat turned up to "high." The Double Win must be practiced by *people*—very special people. Only those who rest fairly secure in their own self-worth need apply. The rest of this chapter will look at four such people: Mary Kay Ash, founder of Mary Kay Cosmetics; William Norris, Chairman of the Board, Control Data Corporation; Marvin Runyon, President and CEO of U.S. Operations, Nissan Motors; and Mo Siegel, CEO (who has an office next to the receptionist and no title on the door) of Celestial Seasonings. Four different personalities with four different approaches, but each practicing the Double Win in his or her own unique style.

Mary Kay Ash: Going Door-to-Door With the Golden Rule

During the depression, a housewife with debilitating arthritis had to go out and earn her living. Lacking confidence and training, she took the only job she felt qualified for: selling household products door to door. She was good at it—so good, in fact, that in a very short time she became an area manager and had several people working for her.

But as her sales rose, she did not. She was held back because she was a woman. So in 1963, she borrowed money, opened a store, and struck out on her own, promising herself and her first salespeople that her company "would be based on the Golden Rule and offer women unlimited opportunities."

This basic Double Win attitude has paid off *beautifully* for Mary Kay Ash and for her fourteen hundred corporate employees and two hundred thousand "Beauty Consultants," independent contractors who now sell Mary Kay Cosmetics in "Beauty Shows" in homes all over the country. Mary Kay is now one of the largest companies in the world headed by a woman.

What's her secret? Some would cynically say it's hype and high-pressure sales techniques that promise saleswomen impossible dreams. Here's how the company newsletter, *Applause,* sometimes overenthuses:

> Driving a pink Cadillac down the street is more than fun—it's a happening. Why not have it happen to you?

Mary Kay is a business in which sales are pursued with almost evangelistic fervor. Each spring in Dallas a huge sales convention is held that rivals the Miss America Pageant with crowning of a sales "Queen" and her court. Thousands of Beauty Consultants gather to be dined (but not wined) and treated to awards like pink Cadillacs which descend from a cloud over the convention stage.

But employees believe the dream. They know that more Mary Kay saleswomen earn over $50,000 a year than women in any other company. *Advertising Age* reports that the 3,391 sales directors (area managers who direct the independent Beauty Consultants) earned an average of $25,000, plus a rental car. And the 31 national sales directors earn an average of $75,000. The true stellar performers, however, are the very top Beauty Consultants, a few of whom earn $250,000 or more a year. Mary Kay has a way of making dreams come true.[2]

But there's another side to Mary Kay, too. It's the poem and personal letter she sent to the brother of an employee who was dying of cancer. It's the corporate offices without titles on the door (your choice of a rug on the floor). It's the sofas in halls and common rooms, and the plants and flowers on every desk from the company greenhouse to add the homey touch. It's the company-supported cafeteria (there's no separate executive restaurant) where every table is covered with white tablecloths and crowned by a vase of fresh-cut flowers.

Gail Daniel, a corporate purchasing buyer, put it this way: "There's a Mary Kay attitude that there are no lower people: Everybody is treated the same." Corporate managers even spend a day each year in the factory so they can experience firsthand what it's like to work on the line.[3]

"Mary Kay is a very female oriented company," Bob Eckelcamp, a data-processing professional, said. "When I was interviewed there were a number of warm and personal questions. Not intimate, but personal. I thought it was the strangest series of interviews I had ever gone through. They were primarily interested in whether I'd fit into the family."[4]

Does this corporate "maternalism" pay off? Apparently so! Mary Kay has been the fastest-growing company in the cosmetics industry for the last decade. It is also a well-managed company with an excellent product line emphasizing skin-care products, which ideally positions it for demographic changes, as the American female population ages.

With the promo, the spring conventions, and the fabulous awards, it's interesting to note what Mary Kay herself thinks is still the key to the success she has shared with tens of thousands of women. Basically, she asserts, it's the "You can do it" attitude which inspired her and which she teaches other women to model.

Asked what she felt was the number-one motivator of women, she replied, "I think men are more motivated by money. For women, recognition comes first, self-fulfillment second, and then pride. Somebody said, if you act enthusiastic, you will become enthusiastic. We try to generate enthusiasm by example."[5]

It's significant that the award that means the most to many Beauty Consultants is not the pink Cadillac or diamond crown, but a small pin in the shape of a bumblebee which is given to sales achievers. Every aerodynamic engineer will tell you that a bumblebee is too big to fly on such small wings. But bumblebees don't know engineering—they insist on flying anyhow.[6] So do Mary Kay's Beauty Consultants—Double Winners built in the image of their never-say-die founder.

William Norris: Profit in the Slums and Prisons

In his mid-seventies, William Norris "makes his living" as Chairman of the Board of Control Data Corporation, a Minneapolis-based firm, ranked number 80 on the Fortune 500 list. Started twenty-seven years ago by Norris himself, Control Data is a $4.3 billion business, dealing in super computers, data services, and peripherals.

So far, it sounds as if there is nothing particularly win-win about CDC, but for William Norris, the corporation is not an end in itself. It also provides corporate capital and energy which can be applied to Norris's particular brand of the Double Win. His goal: achieving social goals in the community which reach far beyond, but which are not in conflict with, the interests of CDC shareholders. Norris's Double Win concept works like this:

Prisons, slums, and classrooms can actually provide profitability centers for the corporation. Equally true is that, along with everybody else, CDC ". . . has a responsibility to be socially responsible."

With Norris at the helm, Control Data has been willing to take risks and make investments in situations that would send most corporations scurrying toward much more likely looking pastures.

While some of his business-establishment colleagues think he is a bit daft, William Norris is always aware of the need to establish the wisdom of any investment in "corporate terms":

> "You have to make it absolutely clear that we are in it for a profit. If you don't say that early, everyone will wonder, 'How is he going to get his money back? Where is he going to rip us off? Where is he going to sneak up behind us?' "[7]

For the past sixteen years, Norris has been able to keep stockholders happy as he has led Control Data Corporation in pursuing a business strategy of applying its computer technology, along with its financial and human resources, to address society's major unmet needs as profitable business opportunities.

Among the major needs Norris hopes to meet are a reduction in unemployment, particularly among disadvantaged youth and handicapped people, along with a revitalization of poverty-stricken urban and rural areas. Control Data attempts to meet these needs by working in partnership with government, business, and local communities.

One of Norris's first socially redemptive but still profitable projects was established in 1968, when Control Data set up an assembly plant in a Minneapolis slum. The plant even included a child-care facility for employees with young children. This experiment did so well it grew into seven "inner city" plants in different parts of the country, which today employ some two thousand workers with payrolls totaling $26 million. All the plants, by the way, are making money.[8]

It's worth noting, too, that Control Data is progressive in many social areas. *Savvy*, the women's magazine, rates Control Data as one of the best companies in America for women to work for because it promotes women to upper management.

Since 1972, Control Data has "loaned" a number of executives to help improve conditions in Minnesota prisons. One example was the establishment of an ombudsman program for the Minnesota State Correction Department, which monitors complaints from inmates, parolees, and citizens. Control Data employees also participate in AMICUS programs, which assist inmates and parolees, and INSIGHT, an inmate-founded and operated nonprofit company inside the Stillwater, Minnesota, prison. INSIGHT helps inmates who work during the day earn college degrees and credits at night.[9]

In 1978, Control Data expanded its efforts to include programs to improve the quality of prison education and training in industry services. Norris and his key executives reasoned that despite large public expenditures, crime and recidivism had not declined among ex-convicts across the nation. Norbert Berg, Control Data Deputy Chairman, puts it this way:

> "If we keep throwing people out of prison who are still functionally illiterate, who have no skills of any kind, they're going to be unemployed and the chances are they're going to be back in prison."[10]

Among some of the practical CDC solutions to this problem are improving inmates' education, training, and future job prospects. Most useful, however, are Control Data's efforts to provide job experience and job training for prisoners, which they can transfer to jobs outside prison after they have been released. For example, in 1981, Magnetic Peripherals, Inc. (MPI), a manufacturing company jointly owned by Control Data along with several other big Minnesota-based corporations, entered into a contract with the Commissioner of Corrections for inmates to work at a computer-component assembly plant inside the Stillwater, Minnesota, Maximum Security Prison. The plant provides inmates with jobs and offers them computer-based education and training in job skills that are in demand by industries around the country.[11]

In the Stillwater project, some sixty-five inmates earn $1.50 to $4.00 an hour building computer components for Magnetic Peripherals, Inc. MPI bought $484 thousand worth of components from the state-owned factory in 1983.[12]

One of Control Data's most intensive efforts in prisons revolves around education and training. A Control Data program called "Fair Break" offers computer-based education and training to over forty correctional facilities throughout the United States. These programs give inmates and parolees individualized, computer-based remedial education along with vocational training and training in job readiness. Key goals are to provide prisoners and former prisoners with life-coping and job-seeking skills.[13]

The Double Wins in Control Data's work with prison and slum areas are obvious. By helping prisoners and ghetto dwellers win, Control Data wins also as it makes a profit. But Control Data's enlightened approach is not limited to outside projects where publicity is readily available. William Norris believes in practicing the Double Win on the inside as well. CDC also operates an "Employee Advisory Resource," staffed by twenty-six counselors who work full and part-time. In addition, "Staywell," a computerized health-maintenance program set up by CDC, has worked so well with its employees that it has been sold to other companies.

Norris feels the same way about programs developed to benefit Control Data employees as he does about investments made by Control Data to improve conditions in the community (as well as make a profit). In both cases, he feels he is only being practical. For example, a Control Data employee who wishes to confront a superior for any reason can do so through a board that includes two of his peers, another supervisor, and an "ombudsman." For Norris, this is just a practical way of minimizing lawsuits, and he adds, "It's a terrible injustice for an employee to be pitted against a large company."[14]

In summary, how can we assess William Norris in light of the Double Win? These factors stand out:

He believes in the basic American philosophy of profit acquired through traditional means.
He has different ideas of how to optimize that profit.
He believes that good people, good citizens, and contented employees all work toward the goal of corporate profit.

I believe William Norris's right to wear the Double Win label centers in his concepts of how to "optimize profit." He wouldn't have to take risks with projects in the slums and prisons, but he does so anyway. By helping the down-and-outers win, he and his corporation win also.

I have a hunch I would like to do business with a man like William Norris every day. He is probably tough at the bargaining table, but I have a feeling I would come away with my share, because Bill Norris is less interested in beating me than he is in seeing that *both* of us win.

Marvin Runyon: Ah So, Y'all

There are indications that in some quarters we are learning from the Japanese. By now, we have all been told that the workers in Japanese companies are happy, and they tend to stay with one company.

At least one American executive is having an unparalleled opportunity to practice the best of Japanese strategy firsthand. Marvin Runyon is President and CEO of United States Operations for Nissan Motors, where he runs a newly built plant in Smyrna, Tennessee, eighteen miles southeast of Nashville. Plans called for having the plant reach full production by late 1984, when it would be staffed with 2,000 human workers and 220 robots.

Runyon has already been in the swing of things, walking the assembly line in work uniform (no one at the Smyrna plant wears a suit or tie). Runyon also shares cafeteria and recreation facilities with other workers and other supervisors. The U.S. Nissan plant bars all perks such as executive washrooms, private dining rooms, and reserved parking spaces. Instead of the typical twelve levels of management, the Tennessee Nissan operation has only five. Says the fifty-eight-year-old Runyon: "We're taking the best of what Japan has to offer and improving on it. Worker input is requested, wanted, and used. We call it Bottoms-Up Management."

Runyon is proud of the fact that assembly-line workers are called "technicians" and that the door to his office is always open to everyone. Runyon's goal is to increase the communication flow from "bottom to top," but he believes he knows where to draw the line:

"It's participative management, not permissive management," he says. "We'd have an awful-looking truck if it was."

The odds against the Smyrna plant producing awful-looking products are long. Nissan spent $60 million over a three-year period to send nearly four hundred Tennessee employees to Japan for a crash course in producing Japanese quality and imitating Japanese corporate life. Many of the Tennesseeans didn't want to come back. Tom Collins, a paint-maintenance manager, said of his Japanese hosts: "They treated us like sons and brothers, although they knew we'd be taking away some of their jobs."

Thelma Ayers, a quality-assurance technician, was impressed with the concern the company had for its employees and vice versa.

Nissan is trying to infuse all of this Japanese spirit into daily routines at the Smyrna plant. Every morning at 7:25, the workers line up for five minutes of light calisthenics, done to the beat of serene Japanese music. Next comes another well-known Japanese practice: small group meetings in which workers are cheerfully exhorted to surpass previously set production records. Workers receive ratings and scores for everything from how well the cars are assembled to how clean they keep the work areas, all of which increases motivation and team spirit.

At precisely 7:40 A.M., chimes send the workers to the nineteen miles of conveyors in the seventy-two-acre Nissan factory. There are two coffee breaks during the day, as well as a forty-five-minute lunch. Fifty-two Ping-Pong tables are busy during the break periods. After work, employees can find additional action on twenty-seven company-sponsored golf, baseball, basketball, and volleyball teams.

Why did Runyon, a former Ford vice-president in charge of thirty-seven assembly plants and 120,000 workers, take on this new challenge, which rose out of former cow pastures in rural Tennessee? He explains: "It isn't often that somebody comes along and says, 'Here's $500 million to start a new company.' It's a great opportunity to start a company from the ground up."

To date, more than 130,000 people have applied for jobs at the Smyrna facility. Tennessee Governor Lamar Alexander calls Nissan "the single most important new industry that ever came to Tennessee." The plant has state officials anticipating a $40 million annual payroll and eight thousand spin-off jobs.

Can Runyon's Tennessee team consistently produce high-quality Japanese trucks, at a planned rate of one pickup every minute? He says, "If they did it in Tokyo, we can do it in Tennessee."[15]

He has traded the traditional labor/management package for a new and different one, which enhances the self-esteem and working morale of all parties, and which clearly embodies the principles of the Double Win. As they say down south, "Ah So, Y'all!"

Mo Siegel: Giving Customers the WIFM

Out in Colorado, there is a young man who, amid almost an "excess of success," still holds firmly to the values implanted in him by significant others in his life when he was a boy.

At age twenty, Mo Siegel started a company he called "Celestial Seasonings." His goal was capitalistically clear: "To make a million dollars by my twenty-fifth birthday." He recalls that he didn't quite reach his original goal. Actually, he didn't hit a million until the first week after he turned twenty-six. Now thirty-three, he heads a company whose sales are approaching $30 million, and he believes they will reach the $100 million mark by 1990. So far, Mo Siegel sounds like a good, tough businessman. He has achieved outstanding results at the bottom line, but where is the Double Win? As we take a closer look, we start to get some hints.

Mo always knew he was destined to be a businessman, but he felt he could be much more useful as a person by being dedicated to health. He noted that, in Europe, herb teas were selling well, but Americans were not using them. Yet there was a growing interest in America concerning good health, fitness, and nutrition.

He recalls that, in the beginning, he would tell bankers, "I am out to build a $100 million company, and I am going to start with selling *herb tea.*" He concedes that most bankers replied something along the lines of, "Have you lost your mind?"

It didn't help when his first products met sales resistance almost immediately. Mo knew that people did not think much of the taste of his product and only drank it when they were sick. He set a goal to manufacture herb tea that tasted good and would be used by people. The product steadily improved, and sales started climbing.

So far, so good. We have a young entrepreneur who wants to build a $100 million company by being dedicated to health and the manufacture of herb tea. But to paraphrase an octogenarian who became famous overnight for her clarion critique of the size of hamburger patties, "Where's the Double Win?" From an interview in the trade paper *Personal Selling Power* come more insights into what makes Mo Siegel tick:

> "There's a battle that I go through sometimes. There is a part of me that clearly wants to make money, big money, and fairly fast. This part of me is motivated by achievement and ambition. The other part is altruistic; the need to do good.

> "I think it's not hard to sell if you are benefit-oriented. I believe that nobody buys anything if there is not a benefit. I always say to our people, 'If you can't give your customer a WIFM—What's In It For Me?—don't show up.' "

At this point, it sounds as if Mo Siegel might be called a "split win" personality. He likes the win-lose idea of making big money fairly fast, but he's also interested in doing good, and giving the customer a good answer to "What's in it for me?" Let's look a little further into what Siegel has to say in that PSP interview, and see if any more Double Win ideas start surfacing.

Mo Siegel can look back to a time when he withdrew an advertising campaign in which his agency compared a new Celestial Seasonings tea with a competing Lipton product. Even *The New York Times* said that, in blind tests, people preferred the Celestial Seasonings flavor by a wide margin. Siegel concedes that it was tempting to blast away at Lipton. All of the marketing research available indicated the wisdom of such a campaign. Go for the jugular in head-to-head win-lose combat. Mo, however, had a different feeling:

> "It took a lot of soul searching to clarify what our real values were. Finally, I decided that I did not want to make a fortune by bad-mouthing anybody. There were so many good things about our products we could say. I could not take it any longer and cancelled the program. I realized that it was a very good decision, which led me to grow further."

Our portrait of Mo Siegel is starting to sharpen in focus. Not wanting to make a fortune by bad-mouthing your competitor is definitely a Double Win Idea. Still, Mo is hardly what you could call a wimp or a pushover. When Lipton introduced a new line of herb teas to compete with Celestial Seasonings, Mo said:

> "I can't stand it and I won't stop improving ours until we beat them. You're right, I am competitive. But I am only concerned with two areas: customer and product. I ask, 'Is the customer happy?' And, 'Are we making the best product?' That's all I care about."

Mo Siegel's strong competitive nature can be explained, at least in part, by his family background. He had a tough and demanding father, from whom he was eventually alienated over differences in beliefs. When the son made it clear he was a Christian, the strongly Jewish father could not handle it and told Mo to make his own way. This may have been a blessing in disguise, because the boy had to make it on his own while confronted with the challenge of maintaining his philosophical ideals. Mo Siegel met that challenge and, in the process, enriched himself and others in many ways.

Mo refers to "many heroes" who inspired him to grow in his business, but admits he draws heavily on the insights of Peter Drucker and Norman Vincent Peale. He listens to educational tapes while riding his ten-speed bike to and from work. In fact, Mo Siegel listens to educational tapes at every opportunity. Olympic skier Billy Kidd, who is Siegel's close friend, swears that he has caught Mo listening to educational tapes while taking his morning shower! Maybe this Double Winner does fit the description that S. J. Guffey, an Associated Press writer in Denver, penned about him: "He's a guy with the moral conviction of Abraham Lincoln, the drive of Lee Iacocca, and the whimsy of E.T."

The portrait of Mo Siegel is starting to fill in now. Obviously a competitor who gives quarter, there is still much more to him than a simple win-lose approach to life. Siegel is a Double Winner and has a value system down on paper to prove it. He comments: "I wanted to establish a value system in our organization so that if I got hit on my bike someday, the value system would stay and the company would do well, based on those values."

Siegel compares his value system to four legs on a stool. The first leg concerns love of the product. Celestial Seasonings is a product-driven company in which the president and his employees seek to develop the best possible product. Siegel says, "To me, it doesn't count how good our products are, but how good they can be. We constantly test our teas with thousands of people a year. We will not let anyone make a better cup of tea."

A second leg in the value stool is a love of customers and consumers. Siegel differentiates by calling his distributors his *customers*. The *consumer* is the end user, the one who buys from the stores serviced by the distributors. He says, "We feel that if we can't sell benefits to the consumer, we shouldn't be in the business. We love to fill consumer needs and benefit people. We are getting over two hundred letters from consumers per week, telling us that we're on the right track."

Mo Siegel believes that if you're not filling needs, you're tricking the people. He would rather die broke and be useful than make all the money in the world selling useless things.

The third leg on the stool is a love of art and beauty. Siegel takes pride in developing new packages for his teas with four-color artwork on each packet. Celestial Seasonings uses some of the best artists in the world for its packaging.

Fourth, and most important for the Double Win, is Siegel's philosophy on the dignity of the individual. While writing this chapter, I had a long phone conversation with Mo Siegel about his dedication to the dignity of the individual. He believes that within everyone is the need for human dignity. Within the company, Siegel tries to meet that need in several ways. For one thing, everyone is an owner at Celestial Seasonings through a stock ownership trust which owns about 10 percent of the company. Already mentioned in an earlier chapter is Siegel's policy which gives any worker on the production line the power to pull a switch and stop everything if he thinks something is wrong.

Siegel says, "My people on the production line have the same dreams and aspirations that everybody else has. They think of things that are good for their families; they think of doing something that is recognized, worthwhile. Their need for all this is no different than mine. Their need for a fair reward for a job well done is no different than mine."

Celestial Seasonings Beliefs

Excellence   We believe that in order to make this world a better place in which to live, we must be totally dedicated to the endless quest for excellence in the important tasks which we endeavor to accomplish.

Our Products   We believe in marketing and selling healthful and naturally oriented products that nurture people's bodies and uplift their souls. Our products must be superior in quality, a good value, beautifully artistic, and philosophically inspiring. . . .

Dignity of the Individual   We believe in the dignity of the individual, and we are totally committed to the fair, honest, kind, and professional treatment of all individuals and organizations with whom we work.

Our Employees   We believe that our employees develop a commitment to excellence when they are directly involved in the management of their areas of responsibility. This team effort maximizes quality results, minimizes costs, and allows our employees the opportunity to have authorship and integrity in their accomplishments, as well as sharing in the financial rewards of their individual and team efforts.

We believe in hiring above-average people who are willing to work for excellent results. In exchange, we are committed to the development of our good people by identifying, cultivating, training, rewarding, retaining, and promoting those individuals who are committed to moving our organization forward.

Our Environment   We believe in fostering an environment which promotes creativity and encourages possibility thinking throughout the organization. We plan our work to be satisfying, productive, and challenging. As such, we support an atmosphere which encourages intelligent risk-taking without the fear of failure.

Our Dream   Our role at Celestial Seasonings is to play an active part in making this world a better place by unselfishly serving the public. We believe we can have a significant impact on making people's lives happier and healthier through their use of our products. By dedicating our total resources to this dream, everyone profits: our customers, consumers, employees, and shareholders.

Siegel believes that if a company concentrates on helping its employees fulfill their needs for dignity, everyone will do very well. He told me about programs at Celestial Seasonings that gave employees opportunities to own stock. They have also developed "venture" teams that work on new and innovative ideas, with people being rewarded for their contributions. Anyone in the company, at any level, can get on a venture team where they know they can make a contribution.

Before we hung up, I asked the Celestial Seasonings president what he thought of the "quid pro quo" philosophy which has the employee saying, "If I do this, the company will give me that." Does this approach really increase productivity? I will never forget Mo's answer:

> "You have to really be filled with the joy of what you're doing. You have to be willing to give without concern about what you're going to get. If I were to say to my production-line workers, 'We don't care about quality, we're putting out a tea product and I want you to crank that product out the door,' what a nightmare it would be for all of them. They would have to go home and have the spouse say, 'What did you do today?' and my workers would have to respond, 'I put out junk.' What kind of dignity is that?

> "But if they feel that everybody is working to make the product better all the time, and that the customers and consumers are happy, then they know they are doing something worthwhile. They feel they have the power to make it good. And there lies the joy and spring and bounce of life."

Siegel told me that he likes to sit down and read letters from consumers which tell him what they think of Celestial Seasonings products. Most of the letters are very positive; some are filled with suggestions for making the product better. Typical letters, however, simply share human needs and concerns:

> I was not doing very well, my doctors told me to get off the caffeine, and so I started using your tea.

> I read that nice quote on the side of your package today and it just put a smile on my lips.

As we hung up, Siegel said, "The letters are the bottom line for me. I get excited. In fact, I get more excited with that than with how much money I'm going to make."[16]

Later, I sat and thought about what Mo Siegel and I had shared in our phone conversation. What is the Double Win all about in any business?

First, you *find a need and fill it* with the highest-quality product or service you can develop.

And then, if the Double Win vaccination really takes, you get excited. You get so excited that you're more interested in pleasing people than in how much money you're going to make. And in any business venture, from giant corporation to hot-dog pushcart on the corner—that's what the Double Win is all about.

LOSERS	WINNERS	DOUBLE WINNERS
Gripe about their failures	Cheer their successes	Share the glory and praise the team

CHILDREN LEARN WHAT THEY LIVE
(Waitley's Paraphrase
of Dorothy Law Nolte's Poem)

Children learn what they live, children live what they learn
If children live with criticism, they learn to condemn
If children live with tolerance, they learn to be patient
If children live with ridicule, they learn to be shy
If children live with encouragement, they learn confidence
If children live with security, they learn to have faith
If children live with fear, they grow up standing at the end of every
    line
If children live with praise, they learn to stand alone and lead their
    parade, even if it's raining
If children are spoiled with indulgence and permissiveness, they
    grow up full of compromise and greed
If children are given challenges and responsibilities, they grow up
    with values and goals
If children live with depression, they'll need a drink, a puff, a sniff,
    a shot, a pill to get them high
If children live with optimism, they'll grow up thinking they were
    born to fly
If children live with hate, they'll grow up blind to beauty and true
    love
If children live with love, they'll live to give their love away and
    become blind to hate
If children are reminded of all the bad in them we see
They'll become exactly what we hoped they'd never be
But if we tell our children "We're so proud to wear your name"
They'll learn to win, believing they'll achieve their highest aim
Because children learn what they live, and children live what they
    learn

What Could It Be Like in a Double Win Home?

Not too long ago I was speaking at an evening seminar for corporate executives and their families. My wife was in the audience and related this story to me after the program.

I had just begun a session on self-esteem and how to build it. She noticed a young boy about twelve, with his head down, sitting next to his father. When I started to discuss the importance of telling your children you love them, the boy perked up and nudged his father with his elbow. Both father and son looked at each other briefly, then the boy sank back in his seat for the duration of the meeting.

After the close, Susan was walking behind them and heard the boy ask his father, "Dad, how come you never tell me you love me?"

The father shrugged him off and said, "The fact that I don't tell you does not mean that I don't love you. I show you by caring for you, giving you a beautiful home to live in, every convenience and every opportunity a young boy could ever dream of."

The boy was silent as they walked out of the hotel meeting room and through the lobby.

That story makes my blood run not cold, but hot. We have covered a lot of territory to this point. We have served up a lot of theory, well sprinkled with anecdotes and examples. But now, as my lecture-tour colleague and close friend Zig Ziglar would say, "We're gettin' down to the short rows." It's time to take the Double

Win out of printed pages and move its heart and spirit into the home, where it's needed like never before. A cartoon from the *New Yorker* magazine says it all in a simple scene depicting a neat, suburban two-story home with attached garage. The punch line? A sign in front reads: "The Krumps live here in a no-win situation."

I doubt that the name of that father and son in my seminar was "Krump," but they were definitely in the no-win mode that is all too prevalent in families today. In this chapter I want to concentrate on describing what it could be like in a home where parents practice the Double Win on their children—and each other.

A Quiz for the Win-Win Parent

Going back to our opening story for a moment, the first question in any win-win quiz is obvious:

"Do you show *and tell* your children they are loved?"

You can never assume your children know they're loved. The father of that twelve-year-old did, and he was well on his way to turning out a son with a self-image thermostat set permanently on zero. Building your child's self-esteem is, perhaps, your chief task as a parent. Here are fifteen more questions to help you gauge your progress:

Is your home a happy, supportive, and loving environment?
Can the occupants hardly wait to come home or hardly wait to leave home?
Is your home full of Double Win role models?
Does each member feel unique and special in his or her own way?
Is it fun at your place?
Is TV viewing monitored or is it a one-eyed baby-sitter and hour-eater?
Is there more cooperation or competition between family members?
Do you have more peace or more war at your house?
Is the labeling process more a buildup or put-down?
Is there more listening or lecturing going on?
Does everyone "pitch in" to help around your home?
Is there an atmosphere of mutual appreciation and respect?
Is there healthy continuity with extended family members (grandparents, cousins, etc.)?
Is there a balance between material and spiritual emphasis?
Is honesty the policy in communication?

Those are fifteen tough questions. I tried to answer them myself as I was writing them and I'm a little uncomfortable with some of the self-revelations. You score each question with one of these answers:

"Total yes," "Mostly yes," "Sometimes," "Not nearly enough."

I counted zero "total yeses," nine "mostly yeses," and six that ranged from "sometimes" to "not nearly enough." I've still got a lot of Double Win homework to do in my own life! That's why it's so important to put these concepts down on paper, so we can think about them and take positive action.

The "Suzuki Method" Builds Better Self-Esteem

After years of studying human behavior and trying to help humans behave more humanely, I am convinced that the secret to successful parenting lies in understanding and developing your own self-esteem and feelings of worthiness. That's just one of many reasons three chapters (4, 5, and 6) of this book are particularly devoted to self-esteem and why it is also mentioned and illustrated in other places as well.

A word of caution and encouragement is due here for all parents. Your own "inner child" of the past may still be programmed more for no-win or win-lose than for win-win (review chapter 4). Don't think your own self-image thermostat has to be hitting the high side of win-win before you can do a good job as a parent. Parenting is an occupation we take with no previous experience. We have to wade in and do the best we can with what we have!

So, take some time to review chapters 5 and 6 and then remember:

Even when you aren't all that sure yourself that you feel you belong . . .

. . . even when you have your own moments of "identity crisis" . . .

. . . even when you feel something less than full of self-worth . . .

. . . and especially when you don't feel chock-full of competence and control . . .

. . . *you can still plant seeds of self-esteem in your children.*

How? By actively demonstrating your love, nourishment, acceptance, and respect to each child on a consistent basis. *I cannot stress the need for this too strongly.* How a child sees himself is what will motivate or discourage him. With a good self-image, he develops high self-esteem. With a bad self-image, he struggles with low self-esteem. Self-esteem is truly the catalyst for your child's failure or success as a Double Win human being.

I realize that sounds a bit frightening to many parents. *What if I blow it?* you're thinking. I understand the feeling. But at our house, instead of worrying about blowing it, we try to do everything we can to succeed. One idea Susan and I have used with great results is the famed "Suzuki method" for teaching children how to master musical instruments, particularly the piano and violin. With the Suzuki approach, teachers have been highly successful in training children as young as two and three to play concertos seemingly impossible for their age.

One Suzuki technique accelerates the learning process for the child by recording a concerto or other musical selection on audio cassette and having the child listen to the tape over and over. With this approach, many children learn to play the entire piece from memory before they can read a note of music!

Our girls Kim and Lisa didn't quite reach that level, but they did learn the piano far easier and faster than they ever had with other teachers.

But perhaps the most interesting—and stimulating—Suzuki idea is this: the parents of the child are taught (before the child is born if possible) not to impose their own limits on the child's talents and abilities in advance. Susan and I have put this principle into action with all the children and it works!

How is it done? One method I use is based on the simulation and self-talk techniques discussed in chapters 5 and 6. To stay aware of my goal to always help and encourage my children, I have recorded short taped messages I play for myself at free moments, while driving or relaxing in my study. These brief messages are full of Double Win thinking and affirming self-talk. Here are several samples I use continually, and which I share with parents in my seminars:

> This is the beginning of a new day. I have been given this day to use as I will for my loved ones and for myself. What I do today is important, because I'm writing a significant page in our lives with

it. When tomorrow comes, this day will be gone forever, leaving in its place whatever I have traded for it.

I show my children I love them every day. I provide opportunities for my children to build their own self-esteem. I accept my children as they are. I am affectionate with my children. I show my appreciation to my children and praise them for specific accomplishments.

I show my children the same respect and consideration I show my friends. I practice the values I preach. I increase their responsibilities and challenges as they grow. I help my children believe in their abilities. I point out things they are good at and things they have done for others. I let my children know they are important members of the family and their opinions have value. I confirm and build my own self-esteem so I can build theirs.

I respect my children's need for privacy. I listen unconditionally to my children. I am consistent in my children's discipline. I let my children go to bed at night on a happy thought. I like myself and am a good parent. I develop my sense of humor and use it every day. The atmosphere in our home is one of love, joy, and cooperation.

You may want to use some of the above paragraphs verbatim, or paraphrase them to fit you and your family more specifically. If you have a tape recorder/player, try recording them in your own voice, over soft music if possible. If tapes are not your thing, put the paragraphs on three-inch-by-five-inch cards and refer to them during the day, while driving, doing dishes, getting ready to go out, and so on.

Telltale Signs of Low Self-Esteem

An ancient Chinese proverb tells us, "A child's life is like a piece of paper on which every passerby leaves a mark." We cannot teach our children self-esteem. We can only help them discover it within themselves by adding positive marks and strokes on their slates.

Low self-esteem characterizes no-win and many win-lose individuals. Following are twelve telltale questions that apply to children exhibiting lower self-esteem:

Do they try to take command of situations in an aggressive manner?
Do they act superior, put others down, and try to straighten out others' faults?
Are they critical of others but unable to take criticism themselves?
Do they get defensive, alibi, justify, and rationalize their own mistakes and defeats?
Are they professional people pleasers?
Do they exaggerate to maintain their own image?
Are they overly impressed by wealth and prestige, and place emphasis on being name droppers?
Do they seem to have a driving need to prove their own self-worth?
Are they procrastinators and unable to live by priorities?
Do they make themselves right by making others wrong?
Are they resentful, complaining, or rebellious of authority?
Can they accept compliments or do they put themselves down when someone praises them?

Any child rating "Total Yes," or "Mostly Yes" to even a few of the above questions is showing serious signs of problems with self-esteem.

When I did the research on these characteristics, I was struck by the fact that I see many adults in positions of authority, high visibility, high income and status, who have similar profiles. Usually, they are takers and not givers. These same characteristics also are common in people who have real problems in contributing and adjusting to society.

Low self-esteem children (or adults) judge their own self-worth by comparison. They have a desperate need for recognition and status. They tend to value things more than relationships. When they lose or do poorly they become resentful. Their tolerance for stress is very low, and they often resort to anger and fear. They try to avoid situations where they might fail.

The High End of the Thermostat

It is vital to plant and nurture the seeds of good self-esteem in your children as early as possible. Since it is a habitual way of looking at life, it is a subconscious reflex that children don't even realize they project. Individuals with high self-esteem have a good feeling about their worth, regardless of their own financial or social status or that of their family.

The Reverend Jesse Jackson constantly refers to self-esteem in his crusades for voter registration throughout the nation: "I am SOMEBODY. I may be poor, but I am SOMEBODY. I may be uneducated, but I am SOMEBODY."

Recently, I shared the speaker's platform with Mr. T., one of the stars from television's "A Team" series, who also co-starred in the movie *Rocky III*. Mr. T. told the audience of young people to get an education, and start contributing to society rather than taking from it.

He ordered them to: "Stop complaining, and start training."

He also reflected: "I may have been born in the ghetto, but there ain't no ghetto in me."

When he looked over at me, I nodded in complete agreement! I believed him, and even if I hadn't been sure, I would have agreed anyway!

All of us have the right to feel that the world was created for us to contribute to, to share in, and to enjoy to the fullest. Children with high self-esteem are more able to:

- admit mistakes and defeats, without feeling inferior
- take differences of opinion without feeling rejected
- accept compliments or gifts by saying "thank you," without self-critical excuses and without feeling obligated
- laugh at their situation, without being self-ridiculing
- feel free to express opinions, even if they differ from peers or parents
- enjoy being by themselves without feeling lonely or isolated
- let others be right or wrong, without attempting to always correct them or ridicule them
- appreciate others' achievements and ideas
- tell a story or talk to others without excessive bragging

Obviously the ratings you're looking for here are "Total Yes," "Mostly Yes," or at least "A good deal of the time." As you monitor your children, ask yourself where *you* stand concerning these same attitudes. You'll find, as I have, areas that may need improvement. But you may also find that both your children and you are doing better than you thought. *Self-esteem is not a static condition.* It is an ever-changing process. The thermostat is always moving up or down based upon the observation base, role-model influence, and the self-talk feedback in response to what is happening in a person's world.

One of the best ways to model positive self-talk for your children in this complicated space age is to help them view the problems of the world as normal ingredients in the process of change. Don't preach about the good old days when you were growing up. Don't fill their ears with griping about the government, the economy, other countries who are less enlightened, and all the disasters that are taking place today. In order for kids to go out and contribute creatively, they need to know that adversity is the mother of invention. Teach them that a Double Winner does not see a crisis as a sure sign of defeat or impending doom; a crisis is simply a form of "intense motivation to solve a problem"!

You can teach your children to be creative by encouraging their dreams and ideas, and by not laughing at their awkward struggles to test and experience new methods, new actions, new people, and new places. Teach them that their problems and setbacks are just temporary inconveniences and learning experiences. Emphasize it constantly: *Setbacks are not failures.*

Armed with a view of failure as a learning experience, children can develop an early eagerness for new challenges and will be less afraid to try new skills. Although they appreciate compliments from others, they benefit most from their own belief that they are making a valuable contribution to life, according to their own internal standards.

The above list of telltale signs of high self-esteem are not simply buzz terms to throw around at PTA or during coffee break with the other mothers of preschoolers. These descriptive lines are goals to be reached through days (and nights), months, and years of patient, faithful nurturing. And, the potential benefits are worth it. High self-esteem individuals usually enjoy good health. They expect and normally get good results from life because they are optimistic and positive. One thing we have especially noticed at our house is that children with high self-esteem make new friends more easily because they think more of sharing *with* their friends instead of what they can accomplish *through* them. This one attitude of sharing with—not getting from—will help free them from the bondage of win-lose thinking and set them apart to become win-win adults in the future.

Parenting Is Like Long-Term Gardening

Always keep in mind that parenting is like gardening. You plant—and you wait. Some seeds take a *long* time to sprout and develop. In my case, my parents planted many seeds of high self-esteem when I was young. Some sprouted early and gave me the confidence to graduate from Annapolis and become a carrier-based jet pilot. Some of the seeds sprouted later, however, when I went on to get training in psychology and become an international platform speaker in the field of motivation and self-improvement. It was then I sorted out the life-changing differences between win-lose and win-win thinking.

I grew up during the post-depression and World War II years in San Diego, California. Like just about everybody else I knew, I recall cutting pieces of cardboard and slipping them inside my shoes each morning so I wouldn't wear holes through my socks at school during the year. My mom and I would laugh when, once in a while, the sandwich I took to school for lunch was two pieces of bread spread with oleo, salt, and pepper. We called it "a chicken sandwich, without the chicken."

I mowed lawns, did gardening, and caddied at La Jolla Country Club so I could buy Mom, Dad, and Grandma birthday and Christmas presents, and save out a few dimes extra for Hopalong Cassidy at the Roxy Theater once a month. We didn't have much money, but we never went to bed hungry and what clothes we had were clean. My parents couldn't afford to give us many *things*, but they gave me the greatest *gifts* I've ever received: *early feelings of self-esteem.*

Mom and Dad both worked. They had their share of personal and financial problems, not the least of which was supporting us three kids. Somehow, though, they always found time to spend with us before we went to bed at night. And that was *quality* time! My mom would read to us and tell us how books could take us anywhere we wanted to go, free of charge. When she presented me with my first library card, it meant more to me than a Michael Jackson video would to any kid today.

Whenever I stop to remember what my mom gave me most of, it certainly had to be the quality and quantity of her time. She listened to my big ideas and I loved to listen to her read to me from her collection of poetry, some from laureates and some from her own pen. Not long ago, I was browsing through some photographs and family memorabilia she had given me after Dad died, and came across a poem she had written for herself shortly after we three children had flown the nest and gone our separate ways. It said so much about building value in our children by taking the time that I want to share it with you:

Where Are My Children?

Have you seen anywhere, a dear boy and a girl, with a much
    younger brother of four?
It was only today that barefoot and brown, they played by my
    kitchen door.
It was only today, or maybe a year . . . it couldn't be twenty I
    know,
They were calling to me to come out and play . . . but I was too
    busy to go.
Too busy with cooking and shopping to play, and now they've
    grown up and wandered away.
If by chance you should hear of a boy and a girl, and their small
    winsome brother of four,
Please tell them I pray, for to see them again, I'd gladly stay hun-
    gry and poor.
Somewhere, I'm sure, they must stop and look back and wish
    they were children again,
And, oh, to be wanted and with them once more, I'd run out my
    kitchen door.
For there's never a task that could keep me away,
Could I just hear my children call me to play.
Where are my children?
I've got time . . . today!

When I finished reading my mom's poem, I realized anew how important her time with me had been. In less than five years, the youngest of our own six children will have grown up and gone off to college. How quickly the transition from child, to parent, to grandparent. The older I get, the more I appreciate the love and time my parents gave to me. I haven't used as much space to talk about my dad, but he shared his time and his philosophy with me, too. After I was in bed he would come to talk with me and when he put out the light to leave, he'd say:

"Son, I've been watching you, and you're about the most special human being I've ever met. I'm proud to wear your name. I missed my ship, but you'll catch yours. I love you, son."

My dad is gone now, but Mom is still around and I see her when I can. God bless you, Dad. And thank you, Mom. I know I was like most kids. I didn't stop to say "Thanks, I love you" enough while I was growing up. But I have a hunch I know what you would say: "Denis, it's all right—just pass the love we gave to you on to your own children."

Self-Esteem Builders for Kids

There are, I know, dozens of books available that talk about ways to love and affirm your children. But if you're like me, you're always looking for one more list that may contain some new thoughts or some good reminders. Here is a list of "positive self-esteem builders" we try to remember—and use—to build Double Win relationships with our children:

The emotional atmosphere in a home, as in a relationship, conveys more meaning for self-esteem than does the content. Nonverbal communication provides the most powerful feedback to the child about how family members regard one another. Make certain your emotional tone matches your spoken word. Let children see positive, warm feelings on your face.

Listen often, without prejudgment, to what they say. This communicates as much love as any endearing words you can use.

If you disagree with something they are expressing or their behavior, recognize their right to feel that way, but let them know your stand. Communicate acceptance of their reasons, but not their actions.

Acceptance is demonstrated by physical contact. Show your affection with a touch, a kiss, or a pat.

Turn the TV off and turn your attention on. Spend time reading, helping, playing, listening, laughing, and exploring with your children.

Find things you can do together, both work and play, fun and learning, sports and religious activities. Let them be part of your life, a significant part. If you don't, they will be wanderers or collectors of things to compensate.

Use frequent and sincere praise. It's better than a gift from a store. The best praise is for specific efforts and in private, rather than in front of siblings. Don't overdo the praise. This can develop into a need that carries over into adult life.

Don't ridicule or criticize children; kindly and quietly counter their efforts to criticize themselves.

Separate the "doer" from the "deed." Teach them to understand that they are not their actions. The behavior is separate from the child. This way they won't grow up carrying their mistakes forward. Failure will be a learning experience.

When expressing your feelings to your children, make certain you use "I" messages, not "you" messages. Say "I feel pleased" or "I feel angry" rather than "You make me feel angry" (or disappointed). This approach does not attack the child's personality and places responsibility for feelings where it belongs, with the person experiencing the particular emotion.

Share your joys and problems with your children. Most of their anxiety is caused by confusing signals from their parents. This sharing promotes security and belonging.

Discover their unique qualities and then help to develop them. Help them feel good about their one-of-a-kind talents.

Encourage them to express their own ideas, even if you disagree with them. Treat them with the same courtesy and respect that you would if they were your best friends.

Make good use of the "teachable moment." You can't teach values at prescribed times. When a situation occurs, good or bad, that has their attention, stop and make applications to their lives and beliefs. For example, help them view a handicapped person as a normal person with special-nurturing needs; or convert a traffic accident on the other side of the freeway into a highway safety lesson.

An important self-esteem quality that shows up in the Double

Win adult is a healthy conscience. Teach your children strong moral values and let them accept responsibilities for their own actions. Help them understand cause and effect, and let them experience logical consequences, as long as they aren't physically dangerous.

Show them alternatives to undesirable behavior and how mistakes might be prevented by thinking out actions in advance.

Teaching responsibility is one of the most critical "musts" in the Double Win. The more responsibility they develop, the better they will feel about themselves. It begins with basic chores as toddlers. It includes picking up and putting away their toys before they can talk. It's learning to put dirty clothes in the hamper and maintain a sense of orderliness. It's teaching them to care about the rights and welfare of others and our society. As they grow older, it includes regular chores and handling money. Most important, they need to learn that they have a choice of how they can emotionally and physically respond to a situation. This is where you set the example: If you say, "I can't help it, that's just the way I am or feel," it will decrease their sense of control or self-worth. If Mom or Dad can't control their emotions, why are the children expected to?

Teach them effective social skills. As their role models, they are watching you relate to others and they learn their good manners or lack of them from you.

Take an interest in who their friends are and make them welcome in your home.

Don't force them to try to live up to your expectations or things you never accomplished in your life.

Don't do anything for your children that they are capable of doing for themselves. Your role is to help them become independent, self-sufficient adults who can share their value with others out of mutual respect, not out of dependency.

Let them experience the thrill of setting and reaching their own goals that you have encouraged them to set.

Don't limit their career aspirations to stereotyped male and female roles.

Give them roots to grow strong with, and wings to fly on their own with.

And most of all . . . love them, laugh with them, and play with them. Too soon, they fly from home, like arrows from the bow.

Our Kids Are Not Xerox Copies

One of the most valuable lessons Susan and I have learned in raising our six children is another basic Double Win principle:

Treat your children with the same respect
you expect from them.

Our children are not Xerox copies of us. Although they mimic us as role models, they cannot be expected to feel or act the way we do. Kahlil Gibran is my favorite on the subject:

Your children are not your children.
They are the sons and daughters of Life's longing for itself. . . .
You may give them your love but not your thoughts,
For they have their own thoughts.
You may house their bodies but not their souls,
For their souls dwell in the house of tomorrow, which you cannot visit, not even in your dreams.
You may strive to be like them, but seek not to make them be like you.
For life goes not backward nor tarries with yesterday.[1]

I talk with many parents who agree with Gibran in principle but, like me, have a little trouble putting it all into practice. Children seem to take so long to learn. They need to be trained, guided, yes, even controlled. I agree, to a point. But sooner or later, depending on the child, a parent simply has to have faith. You have to trust your child. If you want to see your child's self-esteem (and behavior) improve, you have to trust him or her to be responsible (*see* Proverbs 22:6).

Admittedly, that is not always easy, but it is absolutely necessary. One of the saddest sights I see, even in corporate seminar rooms, are adults who were never really trusted by their parents and who have never learned to trust others. Give your children a chance. They will make mistakes. They will fail, but they will learn, especially if you can smile when they mess it up and send them out to try again. Gibran is right: life does not go backward, it goes forward. Yesterday is for lessons learned; today is for living and loving together to build brighter and better tomorrows.

A greeting card someone sent to me says it so beautifully: "Our lives are shaped by those who love us, and those who refuse to love us." Our major goal as Double Win parents is to show our children unconditional love. But that does not mean we can demand love from them. We must earn it, because our children owe us nothing. They did not ask to be brought into the world. We must teach (model) that in order to be loved, you must first be lovable. Our children are the reflection of the faces we see every day in the mirror. I often ask myself, "Is what they see making them smile?"

Marriage: The Ultimate Testing Ground

We talked in earlier chapters about your personal thermostat of self-image and self-esteem. There is another thermostat that controls the emotional climate in your home. If you are parenting with a partner, that thermostat has dual controls. Are your children seeing their parents showing consideration, commitment, and genuine affection for each other? Just as children grow up reflecting how they were treated, so do we—in our adult relationships—flourish or wilt in the emotional environment shared with our intimate partner.

When love is shared by two independent people, with good Double Win, you have what we talked about earlier—synergism. In other words, in a good marriage the combination is greater than the sum of each life. There is a transcendental quality. It is the unspoken, but we know it is there, each of us aware the other is looking for a way to add to the intimacy, to keep the spark, to nurture the fantasy, along with maintaining the mutual responsibilities and trust.

Susan and I know we will have to constantly remind ourselves that to gain this synergism we need to develop more Double Win qualities. So, we continue to look for more ways to enjoy the game, to really make it fun living together. We continue to suppress our egos, earn each other's respect, and keep seeking a greater purpose beyond our creature comforts.

As we have walked and talked about what all this means in practical terms, we have decided that the synergistic qualities we would most like to enhance in our lives are the ones taught us by our youngest daughter's school principal, Dr. Roger Rowe. His philosophy is very simple. He keeps the other person in mind when he communicates. He believes, "If you win, then I win, too." He takes the time to know intimately the interests, the problems, the accomplishments, and the needs of his students.

Any married couple could benefit from Dr. Rowe's mastery of the Double Win communication process. Communication is what the Double Win is all about. That's what relationships are built on.

If I wanted to draft a Double Win motto for families, I could not improve upon the words by Dr. Rowe, shared earlier in this book, but well worth slightly paraphrasing with your partner and children in mind:

> "To be aware of the uniqueness of my loved ones and to treat that uniqueness with loving concern. To encourage my loved ones to develop an 'I will, I can' attitude. To help my loved ones go a step above what they or even others might normally expect. And not be surprised when they do."

Setting the Monarch Free

George Bernard Shaw's marvelous play *Pygmalion* vividly illustrates the importance of this Double Win concept. In the play we witness the amazing transformation of Eliza Doolittle from a flower girl into an elegant lady. Part of her frustration is that Professor Henry Higgins always looks at her as a flower girl. Eliza reflects her insight when she says to Colonel Pickering:

> You see, really and truly, apart from the things anyone can pick up (the dressing and the proper way of speaking, and so on), the difference between a lady and a flower girl is not how she behaves, but how she's treated. I shall always be a flower girl to Professor Higgins, because he always treats me as a flower girl, and always will; but I know I can be a lady to you, because you always treat me as a lady, and always will.[2]

Although the chauvinistic Professor Higgins and the Cinderella-like Eliza are hardly typical role models for today's liberated society, we can learn much from the symbolism in their relationship. For a man and a woman to have a true Double Win relationship, each has to treat the other as she or he would want to be treated. "When I help my spouse win, I win, too."

Marriage offers the greatest potential for practicing the Double Win, as well as the ultimate testing ground. It combines the natural selfishness in wanting another person to fill our longed-for fantasies, with the shared vulnerability of revealing our innermost thoughts, our liabilities, and our commitments.

In chapter 1, with the help of Dr. Aaron Stern (*Me: The Narcissistic American*), we noticed the basic similarities in the win-lose mentality and narcissism, the inborn self-love we must battle all our lives if we are to learn to love others.

In a penetrating chapter on marriage, Dr. Stern points out, "Love always begins as an illusion," which a man and woman create naturally during courtship. "By falling in love with the image of a person before we can know his true substance, we assign him qualities we want to believe he has. In that way we can think of the person in terms that enhance our own lives."[3]

Stern's perceptions are laser accurate. Nearly all of us enter our romantic relationships expecting the other person to provide some kind of magic. Our physical attraction to our mate certainly is filled with this kind of expectation. And so we spend our courtship trying to win the other person over to our side as we play up our most flattering features. Every courtship has its elements of adolescent coltishness and selfishness. It is perfectly natural and adds spice to the relationship.

Stern goes on to share one of the richest understandings of what marriage should be I have ever encountered. He describes, for me, the Double Win marriage when he says:

> Marriage should combine the exquisite excitement of adolescent narcissistic romance with the ability to assume the responsibility involved in caring for each other. . . . The absence of either of these qualities makes the relationship incomplete. These loving qualities supplement each other. Together, they sharpen the sense of fulfillment loving gives us. Narcissistic love is the spice of loving; a more sharing love is its substance.[4]

What Stern seems to be saying is that a little narcissism never hurt any marriage, but he is careful to qualify what he means by "a little." He believes every marriage needs some narcissistic love as the spice to keep romance alive. But he cautions: "Spice is only a seasoning added to a much larger mass of food for flavor; too much ruins the taste of the food that it was intended to improve. Such is the nature of narcissistic love. Small amounts enhance the quality of loving within a marriage. Too much will destroy the marriage itself."[5]

I believe Dr. Stern captures the essence of the true Double Win relationship. In my own marriage, I can sense the tendency to become preoccupied in professional pursuits, financial goals, and the all-consuming challenges in raising six children. I also can see the longing in Susan for a dash of spice in candlelight, slow dancing, and the carefree walks on the beach we shared so often as we chased our own monarch butterfly together.

In maintaining our Double Win relationship, Susan and I have promised each other that we will keep the monarch-butterfly quality in our marriage. We travel together on my business trips at least 50 percent of the time, even though we still have two children at home. We have set aside time alone at Sea Ranch with no phones, no kids, no manuscripts, and no friends, just to experience each other. More walking, less talking about details. More casual activities, less structure. More touching. More music.

As my good friend Harold Hook, Chairman of the Board at American General Life Insurance, puts it, every relationship needs

ALDITS
A Little Difference In The Sameness

Just as it takes effort to nurture children and build a solid business, it takes effort to inject that little bit of difference into your marriage to set the monarch free. Marriage cannot be contained. It must be set free, as two independent persons are able to share all of their values and still maintain the childlike magic of the moment.

It's the Double Win—and it makes all the difference.

THE
DOUBLE WIN
PERSPECTIVE

The Double Win perspective sees the forest *and* the trees. The Double Winner spots opportunities to create synergy by joining individual parts to make a greater, more powerful whole.

The Double Win perspective sees how life intertwines, but can sort out the chaff and keep the real wheat. It can tell the difference between a fad and a trend but not be intimidated by either one, because the Double Winner knows the road most traveled is not necessarily the one to take.

The Double Win perspective is more than relying on luck, fate, or even experience. The Double Winner decides to act and then, with confidence that comes from proper preparation, goes out to achieve the needed results.

The Double Win perspective doesn't curse the darkness because its own light is always bright with hope. It is a balanced, realistic view.

The Double Win perspective does not overlook the struggle through the dark valley and the challenge of the impossible chasm, but it never takes its eye of faith off the summit—where there is always room for both of us.*

*Adapted from an advertisement by Shearson Lehman/American Express.

12

The Grandest Experiment of Them All

As we move through the final decades of this century, many enormous problems and needs stand out: threat of nuclear war, starvation, disease, and poverty are just a few of the more cataclysmic problems that could, as one leading thinker admits, be leading us to the brink of our own extinction.[1] I believe we have another need that may not be as dramatic or well publicized, but which is every bit as important. This need, which is why I wrote this book, can be stated simply:

> We need to change our basic definition of "success"
> and "winning" from win-lose to win-win.

Win-lose thinking continues to catalog short-lived victories, but promises only long-range defeat for our culture. Win-lose must be replaced by win-win or we will all lose.

We have looked at just a small tip of the iceberg of evidence against the win-lose philosophy and its built-in potential harvest of narcissism, hedonism, self-indulgence, and power addiction. We have considered the dangers of the thirst for power and have seen again what Lord Acton realized a century ago and what Adam and Eve discovered in the misty dawn of time: Power tends to corrupt; absolute power corrupts absolutely.

We rest our case against win-lose thinking and living. But there is no time to rest. For quite a few years, "Pogo" has been saying,

"We have met the enemy and he is us." We chuckle, we nod, and we go right on with life, *believing Pogo is right.*

If Pogo *is* right—if the enemy is "us"—we must meet our enemy coming back the other way. Instead of being at war within and among ourselves, which is obviously the win-lose mentality, we must call a truce and agree to try the win-win path to peace.

How? I propose the Grand Experiment: living the Double Win at every level of society, from corporate boardroom to the corner tearoom, from assembly line to scrimmage line. All of us must start to believe, and live, in even the smallest ways, the Double Win idea that:

> "I can no longer simply look out for Number One. I have to look out for you, too, because when I help you win, I win. In fact, we all win together."

It's already happening. Last year, I spoke over two hundred times in top-management meetings, sales meetings, conventions, and rallies of every kind. I believe a new wind of hope is blowing across the land. If you will pardon the pun, it's a Double Wind of awareness and resolve to change our ways and renew and rebuild traditional value structures. Some of the more obvious signs of the times include the following:

The "Search for Excellence" Is Real

As I travel the United States, as well as foreign countries, I see a new mood across all levels and areas of society. Simply put, it is a mood for improvement of methods, techniques, habits, relationships—life itself. One of the more dramatic and conspicuous arenas where this mood prevails is the business world. It is no coincidence that two books illustrating the positive win-win approach to management have recently spent long periods of time together on the best-seller lists.

The One-Minute Manager, by my friends Kenneth Blanchard and Spencer Johnson, helps us master three simple Double Win techniques for managing anyone—including ourselves.

In Search of Excellence, by Thomas J. Peters and Robert H. Waterman, Jr., gives us "lessons from America's best-run companies."

Admittedly, part of the rush to the bookstores to learn how to run our companies and our lives better is motivated by fear and, in some cases, deep concern. In 1960 the United States held 25 percent of the world market share in manufacturing and was the dominant leader in the world marketplace. In that same year, American companies produced 95 percent of the autos, steel, and consumer electronics purchased in the U.S. market.

By 1979, however, our share of world manufacturing was down to 17 percent. American companies were now producing only 79 percent of the autos and 86 percent of the steel purchased in the U.S. market. As for consumer electronics, the share of the U.S. market for American companies had plummeted from 95 percent to 50 percent.[2]

Major cause of our decline was Japan, which grabbed the lead in steel and auto production. I believe Japan has lessons to teach us, not only about management but also about humility and complacency. The Japanese learned from their failure in World War II. They stayed lean and hungry, developing ideas like the Quality Circle, which was introduced in Japan from America!

In the fifties, sixties, and seventies, the Japanese worked on developing Double Win concepts such as employment security, consensus management, and nonadversarial relations with customers and employees. Meanwhile, American companies became fat and sedentary. Win-lose confrontations between labor and management, and a general attitude of trying to get all you can with the least real effort and "too bad for the customer" contributed to the general decline.

But now we're on the way back and, I believe, there's more involved than expense accounts, profit margins, and the bottom line. There is a new awareness of the importance of people and relationships that has been missing in past years. This "people awareness" helps explain the phenomenal success of *In Search of Excellence*.[3] At the heart of   *In Search of Excellence*   are eight basic principles for running an excellent company, which can be adapted in great part for running an excellent anything—family, church, school, club, etc.

In their exceptionally thorough study of sixty-two American

companies, authors Peters and Waterman discovered (perhaps "dusted off" is a better term) truth that has been around for a long time; it just hasn't been used. Now we seem ready to start.

It has been my pleasure and thrill to see this new day dawning in American car companies such as General Motors, Ford, and Chrysler. From 1980 to 1983, GM companies wandered down a long dark tunnel of declining earnings, profits, and morale. When somebody would think he saw a light, it only turned out to be a Japanese freight train coming from the other direction loaded with Toyotas and Datsuns. But in 1984 things turned around. Detroit is looking back on 1984 as its best year in history.

An unpublicized part of the dramatic new scene at GM is being played out at a small, unpretentious inn nestled in the farmlands of Ohio, where groups of General Motors employees have been coming for two-day retreats. Is this special "R and R" time granted by management for exceptional service on the assembly lines? No, in each group are some thirty GM employees, from every department, plant, and level of responsibility. Senior vice-presidents of finance sit coffee cup to coffee cup with installers of dashboards and upholstery.

Only first names are used and no one can describe what he does or at what level of authority. The assignment is the same for everyone: Discuss how to make General Motors a better place to work— how to increase what is called "Quality Work Life."

I have learned that at first labor and management were skeptical about sending union members to talk with executives without a bargaining table between them. But the meetings are producing results. Insights are being gained, along with self-esteem on both sides. Meetings like these at the little Ohio inn are only part of the story that tells of a complacent, self-satisfied giant who became humbled enough to learn from its adversaries. One can make too much of Japanese management principles, perhaps, but I see them permeating American corporations like GM, Ford, and Chrysler. Yes, and with typical Yankee ingenuity, Americans are improving upon what they've learned.

Almost every week, often several times a week, I speak in a corporation setting. Often, before I come on, the executive vice-president, chief operating officer, or marketing director will take a few minutes to give a presentation, usually with visuals, on "Our New Corporate Culture." As we saw in chapter 2, a corporate culture is a company's values, traditions, slogans, etc., summed up in the general concept of "how we do things around here." And one of the key corporate-culture teachings these executives are pounding home is:

Our first responsibility is quality of service to our customer.

Perhaps you are wondering why this is so significant. I believe the significance lies in the simple fact that for years our corporations have paid lip service to the idea of really good quality and good service. Yes, there have been some exceptions like IBM and GE, but across American industry today we are seeing a breakthrough of new concern for looking out, not for Number One, but for *everyone.* Corporation executives are saying it and meaning it for the first time in years, some for the first time! Executives are declaring themselves to their employees and their employees are listening. Dialogue is taking place. I believe all this is a sign that Double Win ideas and principles are taking root and are growing, slowly perhaps, but steadily.

Competition Being Tamed by Cooperation

This is not to say we will cease to enjoy the World Series, Super Bowl, NBA Play-Offs, Wimbledon, or the Masters, not to mention the high school, college, and Olympic competition that is the warp and woof of our national scene.

There will always be a place for competition, in athletics, in business, in life. But what must change is the spirit that turns competition into war and point getting into psychological bloodletting (or worse). In his penetrating critique of our society, Christopher Lasch observes that the free-agent draft, escalating salaries, and promoting instant stardom through the media has caused competition among rivals to degenerate into a free-for-all. "People today," writes Lasch, "associate rivalry with boundless aggression and find it difficult to conceive of competition that does not lead directly to thoughts of murder."[5]

Lasch goes on to mention a study at Columbia University, which revealed that many students hold the general opinion that there can be no competition unless someone gets annihilated.[6]

But it doesn't have to be so. Refreshing examples of competition that is healthy, friendly, and fun surface constantly—even in pro ranks where big money is on the line. Anyone who saw the U.S. Open golf tournament in 1984 saw great sportsmanship in action. When Fuzzy Zoeller, standing on the eighteenth fairway, saw Greg Norman, the big Australian, hole a sixty-foot putt that might have cost Zoeller the Open, Fuzzy waved a towel in mock surrender, thinking that he had to birdie the hole to tie Norman. Then we saw the two of them chuckling and congratulating each other as they faced an eighteen-hole confrontation for the championship.

Zoeller went on to win the play-off by eight strokes—the widest margin to date in an Open play-off. As the golfers strode up the fairways, a commentator said they looked like a couple of old friends out for an afternoon round. Norman, who simply had a horrible day, refused to feel sorry for himself, and Zoeller, as always, displayed his love of the game and his profession. Yet nobody would suggest that Greg Norman had choked, or was "afraid to win." He had won the Kemper Open less than a month before and will win many more. But what Norman and Zoeller showed during the 1984 U.S. Open is that competition can be joyful and friendly and sportsmanship can be more than a nice word. The game of life does not have to be played to "sudden death."

And what about the corporate scene, where the game can be grim and sudden-death play-offs cost people a lot more than first prize in a round of golf? Don Seibert, Chief Operating Officer of the J.C. Penney Company, acknowledges that the idea of competition in business can cause some people to think of cutthroat in-fighting, back-stabbing best friends, and generally ". . . giving free rein to some sort of 'killer instinct.' "[7]

Seibert denies, however, that competition has to be cutthroat in the business world:

> The successful people I know aren't obsessed with beating out the other person and stepping on others' heads to get to the top. Their motivation, instead, is to do such a good job at their assigned task that they come to be regarded as first in a fast field of

excellent talent. In fact, the better your competitors do, the better it makes you look if you win first place. And the ultimate goal in any business is to assemble the best-trained, most highly motivated team in the industry so that as a group you can *all* become first in the marketplace.[8]

Nice theory, but where is it being *worked?* One example is the Nissan truck plant in Smyrna, Tennessee (already discussed in chapter 9). Another illustration of how Americans are *competing* with Japan in a *cooperative* spirit is the new General Motors/Toyota plant in Fremont, California. During 1984, the first of 150 American employees of New United Motor Manufacturing, Inc. (name of the new Fremont operation) were given training in Toyota factories in Japan, where they were strongly impressed by Japanese organization, leadership, and teamwork. One American trainee, who had spent thirty-three years in the American auto industry, commented on Toyota's "great way of doing business." Particularly appealing is the Japanese policy that makes every worker his own inspector, "to make sure that no defect is passed along, but rather taken care of right on the spot."[9]

Can this kind of joining hands across the Pacific be considered "real" competition? A look at the root meaning of "compete" is revealing—even surprising. The Latin source is *competere*, meaning "to come together, agree, be suitable, belong, compete for." Nothing in this original definition of competing suggests the need for a killer instinct. We have added that little feature by coming to believe that excellence can be achieved only at the expense of others.

We have strayed far from the original meaning of *competere*, which speaks of "coming together, agreeing, belonging and competing for." Our narcissistic nature has twisted the real spirit of *competere* which ". . . carries the idea of joining together in a friendly way with other people and then moving jointly toward the same goal—such as putting out a top-notch piece of work for the company," Don Seibert says.

"In the last analysis . . . one person, or a small group of people, have to 'win' in the sense that they do a superior job and move up to a higher level of management. But in the long run, the right approach to competition should mean that everybody is better off just for having run the race."[10]

Self-Esteem Challenges Self-Love

Social critics like Christopher Lasch (*The Culture of Narcissism*) and Aaron Stern (*Me: The Narcissistic American*) have penetratingly analyzed the narcissistic side of our society. Stern sounds a pessimistic note in his last chapter when he observes that the earliest forms of society succeeded—and even flourished—in a struggle for survival that emphasized interdependence and mutual support among all members. Narcissist types (takers) were in the distinct minority because most people were committed to the necessity to be givers—lovers of the group. But as society flourished, more and more people became materially well-off. Today we have a huge middle class that is the most affluent in history. We are also more narcissistic than at any time in history.

Stern feels affluence is not the real problem. What has gone wrong is the failure of many people to stay committed to loving others, to give to the total group, so that all might survive. When survival is no longer an issue, it is tempting to indulge oneself selfishly, and as more and more people succumb to this temptation, there will be fewer givers (contributors to society) and more takers (narcissists). The result, Stern fears, will be that:

> . . . the basic nature of society will change, shifting from a collective effort to a struggle between the takers and the givers. The takers will have their feast, the givers will get stuck with the check—and the price gets higher every day. It will go on this way until the bill becomes unpayable because the majority of us will have become takers. Ultimately, the system will collapse.[11]

Stern's warning, written in 1979, is sobering. Looking back on the riots and rebellion of the sixties and the "if it feels good, do it" binge of the seventies, it is good counsel. To go on with a giggling hot-tub mentality could put society's ship on the rocks. Are we beginning to bring our ship about in the eighties? I believe we are, slowly, to be sure, but the signs are there. While drugs and alcohol are still being consumed at alarming rates, there is a growing awareness—especially among the young—that drugs do not solve problems; neither does soaking nude in the Jacuzzi and consuming multiple six-packs of Lowenbrau.

What *does* solve problems is thinking, praying, and doing what is necessary—in short, be willing to meet your responsibilities and do your duty.

To many sophisticates, that sounds corny and cliché-ridden, I know, but not only is it what we need, it is also the way we are turning because we are getting fed up with win-lose self-centeredness, "meism," and looking out for Number One.

"Where is your proof?" I am often asked. "How do you know there is a shift to be more responsible and duty-bound?" For me, one of the most encouraging pieces of evidence is the result of a national study of perceptions of success, conducted for *Success* magazine by the Gallup organization in 1983. The Gallup people believe their probability sampling procedure represents the adult civilian population, living in private households in the United States (approximately 166 million people). They asked participants in the survey to rate twelve factors of success, such as unlimited money, happy family, a luxury car, enjoyable job, etc. From the twelve factors, they were to choose three they considered most important as criteria for judging personal success. Following is a list, showing how the twelve factors were rated:

Good Health	58%
Enjoyable Job	49%
Happy Family	45%
Good Education	39%
Peace of Mind	34%
Good Friends	25%
Intelligence	15%
Unlimited Money	11%
Talent	7%
Luck	6%
Luxury Car	2%
Expensive Home	1%[12]

This overwhelming vote for the value of health, jobs, happy families, and a good education points to renewed commitment to traditional values that built this country in the beginning. It also points to a society that predominantly wants to give, not just take. People with jobs, family, education, and peace of mind are far more likely to contribute to society than simply take what they can for free.

Another good sign is the growing popularity of two movements many people thought were only temporary diversions. The human-potential movement came, and we glanced up from paying the bills and said, "It's a fad. It will never last. Besides, I'm too busy with reality." The physical-fitness movement came, and we shuddered a bit, shoved our recliners back another notch, and said, "It's a fad. Let's relax until this silly urge to exercise passes."

Both movements have proved us wrong. Both are still here, stronger than ever. Because I have spent a greater part of my life traveling in recent years, I have seen the country from a broader perspective few are able to enjoy. What I see happening is a combination of physical fitness and mental awareness that is adding up to higher self-esteem, higher goals, and a pursuit of excellence at all levels. People are becoming involved in the process of improving their lives, rather than simply living Monday to Friday and hoping for some unexpected pleasure in between.

Today, instead of meeting someone after work at the gin mill, they are more likely to be meeting at the treadmill in the local Nautilus center. Instead of taking a coffee break with a Danish, they may take a fitness break with a quick turn around the block. Instead of a night on the town, many people are opting for seminars, workshops, and study groups offered by their churches, their companies, their local YMCAs or school districts.

We could be poised on the brink of a real breakthrough (breakout) that will free us from the prison of win-lose narcissistic self-adoration and enable us to enjoy a healthy self-acceptance that can reach beyond itself to help others win also. I believe there's a direct correlation between the raising of healthy self-esteem and the reduction of narcissistic self-indulgence that struggles with a poor self-image. Narcissists put high value on self-gratification but low value on themselves.

Beyond Self-Actualization

In a sense, the lifelong path to maturity presents us with repeated tests of our readiness to give up and give away. The narcissist clings to the bits and pieces of his lightly valued self, unwilling to give and move on. The Double Winner understands that the more he or she gives up, the more he or she can gain.

With the strength of mature self-esteem supporting them, Double Winners can put themselves on the line. They can give where necessary and sacrifice with only the possibility of eventual "return on investment." Double Winners don't keep score. They know that as they give of themselves unquestioningly, they will reap tenfold results, be it in the short or long run. They are secure enough in their sense of what they are worth and who they are to give up and give away.

When I can feel *that* secure, when I am able to give up and give away to help the other person win, I reach a new summit on the scale of values. Abraham Maslow's "hierarchy of needs" is well known. We start with basic physiological needs—eating, drinking, and sex—and then move up to safety needs—security, stability, dependency, freedom from fear, the need for structure, order, and law. From there we go to the needs to belong and be loved, followed by the needs for esteem. Maslow divides esteem needs into two subsidiary parts: (1) strength, achievement, adequacy, competence, and independence; (2) reputation, prestige, status, fame, glory, importance, and dignity. Finally, at the pinnacle of the hierarchy is the need for self-actualization—realizing your full potential by becoming all you want to be (self-fulfillment).[13]

Maslow's hierarchy certainly makes sense. It is natural for a human being to progress from basic physiological needs right on up through esteem to self-actualization, but is that as high as we should go? I agree with Michael Maccoby's observation that while concentrating on self-actualization, I can ignore or be unaware of self-centeredness and egocentrism. In his book *The Gamesman,* Maccoby writes:

> To develop the heart, one must open it to others. Maslow considers the highest need "to become everything that one is capable of becoming," but this is naive if it assumes that all possibilities are moral and can coexist. We are all capable of good and evil, of being lovers and murderers, wise men and women or madmen. We also may be capable of developing many talents and roles, from artist to athlete, beachcomber to manager. The point should not be

that by satisfying lower needs, we automatically develop higher needs, but rather that we must choose who and what we will be and strive toward actualizing innate capacities for reason and love by overcoming greed and egocentrism, at the same time developing competencies that are socially productive and talents that are life enhancing.[14]

In other words, the Double Win is not in our human nature, it is in our nurture. Much of this book has been devoted to your self-esteem and, yes, your self-actualization, but obviously both can be a natural part of the win-lose approach. The Double Win goes beyond self-esteem and self-actualization to a nurturing attitude that we gain as we learn to give, not take. Taking is win-lose behavior. Giving is win-win. Givers are not concerned primarily with "quid pro quo"—getting something for something. Givers give because it is the right way to do business in a hurting world that is jaded and dazed from being exploited and ravaged by takers.

The takers are the narcissists, the win-lose competitors who want to have it all, but who never get enough. The givers are loving people, the Double Winners who want everyone to have some, because they realize that if you are a true giver, some is more than enough.

Be a taker and your self-image thermostat will stay stuck on low. You may cover it up, even climb to the top of the win-lose heap. You may gain prestige and esteem; you may become powerful, confident; you may even reach what you believe is your "full potential." But inside you will always know exactly what your thermostat says.

A vividly tragic example of a taker with his self-image thermostat stuck on low-low was the young man Adolf Hitler. But he persevered. I suppose you could say he displayed qualities of an unenviable kind of "winner" as he rose from paperhanger to fuehrer. First he convinced a few gullible and desperate followers that he was destined to lead Germany out of economic chaos into world dominance. Then he projected a fanatic air of self-confidence to the masses through radio loudspeakers. With carefully calculated words he distorted the expectations of an entire nation and fanned the fires of hatred among people who normally would have ignored his raving.

Adolf Hitler was a pathetic example of the "I'll do it to others *for* myself" philosophy. His bluster and seeming charisma was a gigantic bluff to hide a miniscule self-image weighed down under a crushing load of self-negation and guilt. He won his share of victories, but at terrible expense to millions. In the end he lost the entire ball game and became one of the great takers in modern history, perhaps the greatest taker of all time.

I confess that one of the happiest days of my life was June 6, 1944, my eleventh birthday. I'll never forget the smile on my mother's face when she showed me the morning paper and said, "Happy D-Day, Denis, my son. The Allies have invaded Normandy." For the rest of my growing-up years I identified D-Day with Denis's Day and have often pondered how the beginning of Hitler's end came on my birthday.

Be a giver, however, and your self-image thermostat will inevitably rise to a comfort zone where you can function with joy and satisfaction for your own good and that of others. As the New Testament puts it, you can love your neighbor and yourself.[15]

The Double Win Philosophy

As I've written this book it has occurred to me at several points that I could easily be accused of advocating some sort of one-world Marxist collectivism, which practically obliterates the individual's personality and creativity. This is not what I intend or believe. Cornerstones of my personal Double Win philosophy are these:

1. Individual creativity and entrepreneurship, which is the seedbed for growth and progress. It is no coincidence that the companies and corporations we have noted throughout this book who practice Double Win principles are the innovative firms who are always seeking new ways to do it better.
2. Competition tempered with cooperation, a Double Win principle that is the safeguard of quality, reasonable prices, and fair play in the marketplace as well as a prime motivator of personal excellence in any endeavor.
3. The right to do it differently, act differently, be different in a unique effort to be the best in order to give the best, which leads to the Double Win.

When I trace back to find the roots of my personal philosophy, I inevitably arrive in my room as a young boy with my dad saying good night. In addition to always telling me what a special human being I was, he would often go through his little ritual of leaning back against the light switch by the door and rubbing against it to "magically" blow my light out. And he'd often say:

> "I'm blowing your light out now and it will be dark for you. In fact, as far as you're concerned, it will be dark all over the world because the only world you ever know is the one you see through your own eyes. So, remember, son, keep your light bright. The world is yours to see that way. I love you, son. Good night."

I have never forgotten my father's graphic way of teaching me about perception and the eye of the beholder. What he was telling me about the light is that I have the power to keep my corner of the world bright. It all depends on how I want to look at it.

I would like to offer you my father's bit of wisdom in the hope you can take it into whatever walk of life is yours this day. In an earlier chapter I mentioned that I would try to illustrate the win-win philosophy with examples from the world of sport, the business world, and in any other walk of life where I could discover the Double Win in action. I've tried to do that, but I am acutely aware of something else I said earlier as well: most of the real Double Winners go unsung and unnoticed. They are the "average" people who might appreciate what Olympic track star Wilma Rudolph once told me: "Just because I won three gold medals and am looked upon as a world-class athlete . . . that doesn't make me a world-class person."

I like that. What Wilma was saying is that a world-class person is the one who makes the effort and takes the time to do the things that others only give lip service to. There are vast hosts of world-class Double Winners who don't make headlines, who aren't interviewed on "Good Morning, America." They are too busy giving as they go about the business of living the Double Win. They aren't making news because they're too busy making the Double Win work!

As I have been writing this book, people have constantly asked, "The Double Win? What's it about?"

I smile and reply, "It's the Golden Rule in anything from a three-piece suit to a jogging suit, from a hard hat to a homemaker's apron, from Levis to Calvin Kleins."

No matter what "uniform" you wear each day, you can go for the Double Win. It's an exciting, satisfying game with very few rules:

Treat others as you want them to treat you.
Help others win and you win also.

The Double Win is simple. I only wish it were easy.

Epilogue:... Butterflies don't hit it too hard

The sun hung just above the water on the horizon like a bright melon ball. "Strange," I mused, "how it takes all day to move in a giant orbital arc from east to west, almost unnoticed. And then, like a surrealistic, orange hot-air balloon—weary of flight—it cools and settles rapidly beneath our view, in scarcely more than a minute, leaving us violet, pink, gray, and magenta memories of its passing."

Sunset is a marvelous time to walk on the beach and clear one's senses. And my mind was anything but clear at the moment. It had been difficult enough trying to make my final case in the last chapter of *The Double Win* without having to figure out how to get it converted from "green glitches" on my Apple II monitor into hard copy from my daisy wheel dot and matrix printer. During the past forty minutes I had unintentionally perforated, torn, and mutilated the table of contents and most of the footnotes trying to "print out" the text from my floppy disks.

I also chastised myself for having been so foolish as to believe I could easily write a nonfiction work of this complexity at our ocean retreat. The seaside is more for reflecting, and reading and writing lighter or more inspirational stuff, rather than grinding out philosophies on self-esteem and strategies of management.

"Free verse and haikus might flow in this environment," I admitted, "but not the nine skill areas in the Double Win."

Fortunately, I had brought along Anne Morrow Lindbergh's *Gift From the Sea*. I had been dipping into it between intense sessions on my own chapters—much to my relaxation and benefit. I had telephoned Mrs. Lindbergh—years before—to tell her how much I enjoyed her work. Like the seashore, it is casual, unpretentious, and revealing.

As I made my way down the rocky bluff onto the stretch of beach in front of our house, I gazed northward and caught my breath at the splendor of the sun's afterthoughts, with hues that stretched as far as I could see. *How fortunate I am*, I thought, *to be able to step out of the clutter of hotel meeting rooms, airport waiting lounges, baggage-claim areas, and neon lights, into this wonderful setting.* The wet sand felt good between my toes. It didn't matter that I had forgotten to roll up my pant legs, and they were getting soaked by the rolling surf. I'd always forgotten to roll up my pants when I was a boy—why change now? As I walked, I kept thinking about Anne Lindbergh's profound wisdom in *Gift From the Sea*.

"There is a Double Winner," I said aloud. She had been married to the most famous American of the century. They had suffered the greatest possible tragedy in the loss of their young son. And through the years, she had rebounded and grown to share the depths of her soul with all of us through her inspirational writing. She never sounded bitter. No, she was always exuding optimism and caring. Like every kindred spirit of the Double Win, Anne Lindbergh was more interested in sharing her values than in baring her wounds.

As I moved up the beach, out of sight of the house, the colors of the sunset faded into slate gray. As if a huge curtain in the sky had opened, the stars made their first appearance of the evening. I stopped and sat on a large piece of driftwood to compare my recollections of Anne Lindbergh's book with Double Win ideas. She had spoken of five seashells. I inventoried those shells in my memory and smiled as I began to sense some analogies.

The channelled whelk, she had written, is about the size of one's thumb and spirals to a point at one end. The whelk is an ideal place for a hermit crab to call home. The hermit crab keeps life simple, moving on, not trying to possess. That was the Double Win idea here. Worldly possessions can come and go. They are not guaranteed.

The treasures in life that are real are not the ones we strive for materially. Real treasures can be seen in a sunset . . . or in the magic of a tidal pool . . . or when you throw a Frisbee and watch your Labrador retriever leap and catch it . . . or when you run in the wet sand and get your legs tangled up with your grandson's, giggling as if you were a playmate again.

Like the channelled whelk, the Double Win is simple. Success cannot be possessed, only shared. "If you win, then I win, too!"

Her second subject, which houses the sea snail, is called the moon shell. It's a blue-gray spiral that circles out from the center, about the size of a silver dollar. She described it as a self-contained moon or island. When I thought about it, it reminded me that every man and woman is an island in a common sea. All of us must be happy within ourselves, with inner peace and internal values, before we can stop needing to take from others to be gratified. The solitary moon shell teaches us that we must get in touch with ourselves first, before we can ever touch another person with love and with meaning. Self-esteem is the prerequisite for the Double Win.

As I remembered the third shell from *Gift From the Sea*, I also thought of my special friend the monarch butterfly. The double-sunrise looks like two beautiful, symmetrical butterfly wings, touching each other in one tiny joint. Gold with blue on the edges, this exquisite shell symbolized—to Anne Lindbergh—the perfect physical relationship between two people. How fragile our love is for one another. How easy it is to break one side or crumble off a tip.

I thought about the double-sunrise shell and the Double Win, and how similar they are: both sensitive and delicate. I vowed to keep my precious relationships intact and whole by communicating with the "I'll make them glad they talked with me" attitude. By keeping the other person in mind, I can make my marriage and my business transactions flow as a two-way street.

I got up off the driftwood and started south, back toward the house. Susan would be expecting me for dinner soon. My mouth watered at the thought of fresh abalone from our own grotto, with salad and baked potatoes. I could think of nothing I loved more than Sunday-evening dinner with my family.

Anne Lindbergh's fourth shell—the oyster—was a lot like our family. We have been through all the trials, tribulations, and exhilarations of most families. The oyster analogy was a good one for me, I concluded. Uneven growth, struggling and groping. What a long process it had been for me to mature out of the narcissistic win-lose jet set in my twenties and thirties toward an understanding of the Double Win as a way of life. As simple as the concept of the Double Win appears, it takes real effort to live it. Like the oyster, it develops in the bedrock of a family, or a company, or any other relational setting, fiber upon fiber, year after year, until it is very difficult to pry loose. This Double Win growth is not experienced without constant work, patience, and commitment. But how strong it is, with the bonus of a pearl inside, formed by all the irritations, stresses, and challenges of life.

I began to jog leisurely as I came up from the beach to the dirt path that winds back to our hideaway by the sea. I had about a mile to finish my analogy between seashells and the Double Win. Anne Morrow Lindbergh's Argonauta, or paper nautilus, would be a challenge. Her fifth shell was named after Jason and the Argonauts, who went in search of the Golden Fleece.

The Argonauta is a thin, waferlike membrane that looks like a miniature honeycomb. It is like a ship that carries a mother sea urchin and her offspring up from the bottom of the ocean and out on their own to seek their fortunes. And as they all wash out of the Argonauta to new horizons of growth, they each go a different way. The Double Win is different for each of us. Each of us must ask what it means to us and then set specific goals to help us reach our ports of call. Instead of the Golden Fleece, we may want to concentrate more on the Golden Rule, which my good friend Hans Selye had reworded: "Earn Thy Neighbor's Love."

I could see the smoke curling out of our chimney as I opened the grape-stake gate that had kept the sheep from wandering in decades past. I looked forward to putting on some dry jeans and getting as close as possible to that fire.

It was time to put *Gift From the Sea* and the five little shells back on the bookshelf until our next encounter. I wondered what the macho men who read *The Double Win* would think about an ex-navy carrier-based pilot who quotes Anne Morrow Lindbergh? *Well, never mind*, I shrugged. *I enjoy quiche, too!*

The children were helping Susan set the redwood picnic table on the enclosed porch as I walked in, padding across the tile floor in my wet socks.

"We thought you got lost," Susan teased. "The boys were about ready to organize a search party."

"It was such a beautiful sunset, I decided to spend a couple of hours just relaxing and meditating," I responded.

"You really need to stop and smell the roses more," she said. "You've been hitting it hard lately."

I went in and sat by the fire. I hoped I could honestly believe that I was learning that "hitting it hard" and "chasing it" were philosophies to be discarded like a caterpillar sheds its cocoon to become a monarch butterfly. Butterflies, I remembered, don't "hit it hard"; they float with a light touch.

As I studied the faces of my beautiful wife and our six children, I realized it was Father's Day. I marveled at the individuality and uniqueness in each of our children. Like monarch butterflies, all but two of them were flying free on their own. What a joy for all of us to be together again, if only for the weekend.

We sat down to our meal and as I finished saying grace, I added a silent thank-you of my own to God for teaching me that the greatest gift a father can receive is in giving his love to his family.

Before the fire burned low, I promised myself, I would let each of them know how rich I was from sharing in their lives. And I would pen these thoughts:

Sharing . . . caring . . . giving . . . receiving. Getting the most out of life as we give our best to others.

The Double Win!

There is no greater joy for me
Than moments with my family.
Those early years with just us two,
So young and free, with love so new.
Our firstborn came and we numbered three
In this circle of love called Family.

We wondered what we'd ever done
Without our precious little one.
We'd skip and run and laugh and play,
Hoping that we'd always stay
This young, right now, and time would stop
And not grow up and run away.

Gold medals and diamonds can never replace
The sparkling glow of my Family's face.
There's nothing I would rather do
Than fire up the barbecue.
Hot dogs, six kids, and holding my wife,
These are my riches, gems in my life.

I've traveled the world, to the seven seas.
I've been up at the top, and down on my knees.
I've fretted, I've struggled and misunderstood.
I've worried, and taken for granted the good.
There've been bee stings, and dog bites, and crocodile tears,
And Thanksgivings, and red kites, and plentiful years,
And Sunday with Grandma, and Easter's rebirth,
And trimming the tree with holly and mirth.

Now when evening appears and the shadows grow,
The candles flicker, the music is low,
The computerized toys have been put away,
Little girls and boys have called it a day,
I reflect where I've been, where I'm going to be,
But wherever I look, I always see
That part of my heart so important to me.
Thank You, Lord, for my Family.

Notes

Chapter 1

1. Robert J. Ringer, *Looking Out for Number One* (Beverly Hills, Ca.: Los Angeles Book Corp., 1977), p. 10.
2. Ibid., p. 33.
3. Ibid., pp. 33, 34.
4. Ibid., pp. 34, 35.
5. Examples of these books include: *Twenty-five Steps to Power and Mastery Over People* by James K. Van Fleet; *The Magic of Getting What You Want* by David J. Schwartz; and *Molloy's Live for Success* by John G. Molloy, who also wrote *Dress for Success* and *The Woman's Dress for Success.*
6. Aaron Stern, M.D., *Me: The Narcissistic American* (New York: Ballantine Books, 1979), pp. 13, 14.
7. Ibid., p. 123.
8. Ibid.
9. Ibid., p. 126.
10. Terrence E. Deal and Allan A. Kennedy, *Corporate Cultures* (Reading, Mass., Menlo Park, Ca.: Addison-Wesley Publishing Co., 1982), pp. 41–43.
11. Leslie Wayne, "ITT: The Giant Slumbers," *The New York Times*, July 1, 1984, pp. E1, E21.
12. Deal and Kennedy, *Corporate Cultures*, p. 43.

Chapter 2

1. Dr. Jonas Salk, for whom I worked for many years at the Salk Institute for Biological Studies, makes a similar statement in *Survival of the Wisest.*
2. *The Olympic Games* (Athens, Greece: Ekdotike Athenon S.A., 1976).
3. Terrence E. Deal and Allan A. Kennedy, *Corporate Cultures* (Reading, Mass., Menlo Park, Ca.: Addison-Wesley Publishing Co., 1982), p. 4.
4. Ibid., pp. 6, 7.
5. Ibid., pp. 8, 9.

6. Ibid., p. 9.
7. Ibid.
8. Ibid., p. 7.
9. Ibid., p. 13.
10. Ibid., p. 56.
11. Ibid., p. 49.
12. Ibid., p. 16.
13. Ibid., p. 45.
14. Robert J. Ringer, *Looking Out for Number One* (Beverly Hills, Ca.: Los Angeles Book Corp., 1977), p. 38.
15. Ibid., p. 38.
16. Ibid.
17. Quotes by Phil and Steve Mahre taken from a report in *The New York Times*, February 20, 1984, p. C6.

Chapter 3

1. Dorothy J. Gaiter, "Helping the Handicapped Up the Ladder of Scouting," *The New York Times*, April 25, 1984, pp. C1, 10.
2. *Bugei Shunju* magazine, April 9, 1984. Translated by the Asia Foundation's Translation Service Center. Author, Makoto Kikuchi, Director of Sony Corporation Research Center.
3. Sparkle Stiff, "Super Schoolmaster," *Ranch & Coast* magazine, October 1983, p. 29.
4. See Wayne Dyer, *The Sky's the Limit* (New York: Pocket Books, a division of Simon & Schuster, 1980), p. 329.
5. Ibid., p. 330.
6. Ibid.
7. Roy S. Johnson, "Richardson Starting to Regain Respect," *The New York Times*, April 16, 1984, p. C5.
8. Daniel Goleman, "The Faith Factor," *American Health*, May 1984, p. 51.
9. Ibid., p. 54.
10. Attributed to Father Keller, founder of The Christophers.

Chapter 4

1. M. Scott Peck, *The Road Less Traveled* (New York: Simon & Schuster, 1978), p. 53.
2. See Proverbs 23:7.

Chapter 5

1. See Dave Anderson, "The Captain Is Saluted," *The New York Times*, March 5, 1984, p. C6.
2. Terrence E. Deal and Allan A. Kennedy, *Corporate Cultures* (Reading, Mass., Menlo Park, Ca.: Addison-Wesley Publishing Co., 1982), p. 11.
3. Thomas J. Peters and Robert H. Waterman, Jr., *In Search of Excellence* (New York: Harper & Row, Publishers, Inc., 1982), p. xix.
4. Kenneth Blanchard and Spencer Johnson, *The One-Minute Manager* (New York: Berkley Books, 1981, 1982), see especially pp. 65–98.
5. *The New York Times*, August 20, 1981, p. 3.
6. Peters and Waterman, *In Search of Excellence*, p. 158.

7. Ibid., p. 123.
8. Curtis Hartman, "Who's Running America's Fasting Growing Companies," *Inc.* magazine, August 1983, p. 46.
9. Tom Richman, "One Man's Family," *Inc.* magazine, November 1983, p. 151.
10. Ibid., p. 151.
11. Ibid., p. 156.

Chapter 6

1. Donald Griego, "Speed Skier," *US* magazine, May 21, 1984, pp. 68, 69.
2. From interviews on "CBS Sports" and "Good Morning America."
3. Thomas J. Peters and Robert H. Waterman, Jr., *In Search of Excellence* (New York: Harper & Row, Publishers, Inc., 1982), pp. 58, 59.

Chapter 7

1. Irving Dardik and Denis Waitley, *Quantum Fitness* (New York: Pocket Books, a division of Simon & Schuster, 1984), pp. 88, 89.

Chapter 8

1. See Galatians 6:7 in the New Testament.
2. For information, write to Books on Tape, P.O. Box 7900, Newport Beach, CA 92660. You will receive an information packet on request.
3. Earl Nightingale, *Direct Line 13* (Chicago: Nightingale Corp., 1974), p. 1.
4. Ibid.
5. Ibid.
6. E. Jacobson, *Progressive Relaxation* (Chicago: University of Chicago Press, 1942).
7. Irving Dardik and Denis Waitley, *Quantum Fitness* (New York: Pocket Books, a division of Simon & Schuster, 1984), p. 90.

Chapter 9

1. Carolyn Jabs and Caryl Avery, "How Winners Win," *Self* magazine, May 1984, p. 119.

Chapter 10

1. For a more complete list, see the chart on p. 187 of *In Search of Excellence* by Thomas J. Peters and Robert H. Waterman, Jr. (New York: Harper & Row, Publishers, Inc., 1982). Many additional firms are also named throughout the book. For another list of well-run companies where the Double Win can be found in use, see *Corporate Cultures* by Terrence E. Deal and Allan A. Kennedy (Reading, Mass., Menlo Park, Ca.: Addison-Wesley Publishing Co., 1982), p. 7.
2. Robert Levering, Milton Moskowitz, and Michael Katz, *The 100 Best Companies to Work for in America* (Reading, Mass., Menlo Park, Ca.: Addison-Wesley Publishing Co., 1984), p. 201.
3. Ibid., p. 200.

4. Ibid.
5. Gerhard Gschwandtner, *Superachievers: Portraits of Success* (Englewood Cliffs, N.J.: Prentice-Hall, Inc., 1984), pp. 33, 36.
6. Terrence E. Deal and Allan A. Kennedy, *Corporate Cultures* (Reading, Mass., Menlo Park, Ca.: Addison-Wesley Publishing Co., 1982), p. 40.
7. From article in *Express* magazine, November 1983.
8. Ibid.
9. Information obtained from Control Data Fact Sheet, released April 1984.
10. Don Clark, "New CDC Unit Aligns Educational Ventures," *St. Paul Pioneer Press,* Wednesday, February 1, 1984.
11. Control Data Fact Sheet.
12. Don Clark, "New CDC Unit . . ."
13. Control Data Fact Sheet.
14. From *Express* magazine.
15. Michael J. Weiss, "Ah So, Y'all," *American Way* magazine, May 1984, pp. 120–122.
16. Besides a telephone conversation, information on Mo Siegel obtained from Gerhard Gschwandtner, "The Celestial Salesman," *Personal Selling Power,* pp. 10–12.

Chapter 11

1. Kahlil Gibran, *The Prophet* (New York: Alfred A. Knopf, 1972), p. 17.
2. George Bernard Shaw, *Pygmalion,* quote from *Selected Plays* (New York: Dodd, Mead & Company, 1981), p. 589.
3. Aaron Stern, M.D., *Me: The Narcissistic American* (New York: Ballantine Books, 1979), p. 110.
4. Ibid., p. 111.
5. Ibid., p. 116.

Chapter 12

1. "A Conversation With Jonas Salk," *Psychology Today,* March 1983, pp. 50–55.
2. John Naisbitt, *Megatrends* (New York: Warner Books, 1982), pp. 55–56.
3. Thomas J. Peters and Robert H. Waterman, Jr., *In Search of Excellence* (New York: Harper & Row, Publishers, Inc., 1982).
4. Christopher Lasch, *The Cultures of Narcissism* (New York: Warner Books, 1979), p. 208.
5. Ibid.
6. Donald V. Seibert and William Proctor, *The Ethical Executive* (New York: Cornerstone Library, a division of Simon & Schuster, 1984), p. 20.
7. Ibid., pp. 20, 21.
8. Sam Jameson, "U.S. Trainees Praise Toyota System," *Los Angeles Times,* Tuesday, June 19, 1984, Part 4, pp. 1, 5.
9. Seibert and Proctor, *Ethical Executive,* p. 21.
10. Aaron Stern, M.D., *Me: The Narcissistic American* (New York: Ballantine Books, 1979), p. 193.
11. "What Is Success?" *Success* magazine, October 1983, p. 47.
12. For a thorough description of Maslow's hierarchy, see Abraham Maslow, *Motivation and Personality* (New York: Harper and Row, Publishers, Inc., 1954), pp. 39–46.
13. Michael Maccoby, *The Gamesman* (New York: Simon & Schuster, 1976), pp. 223, 224.
14. See Matthew 22:37–40.